The Money Game 101

S. S. CLARK

This publication is designed to educate and provide general information regarding the subject matter. However, laws and practices often vary from state to state and are subject to change. Because each factual situation is different, specific advice should be tailored to the particular circumstances. For this reason, the reader is advised to consult with his or her own advisor regarding that individual's specific situation.

The authors have reasonable precautions of this book and believe the facts presented in the book are accurate as of the date it was written. However, neither the authors nor the publisher assume any responsibility for any errors or omissions. The authors and publisher specifically disclaim any liability resulting from the use or application of the information is not intended to serve as legal advice related to individual situations.

ISBN: 0615635199
ISBN 13: 9780615635194

Library of Congress Control Number: 2012907404
Embraceink, Philadelphia PA

ACKNOWLEDGEMENTS

I'd like to give praise and thanks to the Lord, The Almighty. To my family and friends that were instrumental in me being nurtured into the man I've become. My old head Nate Swint for always being authentic. To the people that gave me assistance that made this project possible...My threshold Alisha, my man Fella, and all those that pushed me to complete this work. To my children and my BFF Sheree...Special thanks to Angeline...and Mrs. Loretta for being able to love me as her own without judgment. Troc for being there during some difficult times. To my roots on the Dub and all those who turned it around and gave a positive contribution. To the youngster Bean for his drive to keep everyone together as a family. To all the people that came from humble beginnings that had the courage to turn things around after being caught up in the rat race called life.

TABLE OF CONTENTS

BIRTH OF THE IDEA

I had just returned to the United States after having spent some months in Germany when I noticed several changes had taken place. It seemed that each time I ran into anyone from my old neighborhood and engaged in small talk, the topic would shift to how things were going from bad to worse.

I have to admit; at first I was skeptical because of how often you hear someone from the hood say things are tight. In the hood, people complaining about times being rough is as commonplace as someone informing you of who won the lottery.

The depressing vibe felt unfamiliar after living in Germany, where things seemed to be heading in a more positive direction. I could not quite put my finger on it. To be honest, I just made a mental note of it, placing it at the back of my mind.

After a few days of getting up to speed back in the States, it was time to check on my twenty-year-old son and his mother. I never had that open relationship some fathers have with their sons. For the most part, my son is a pretty good kid. However, he often displays an aloofness neither I nor his mother had when growing up.

Not to get too deep into my personal affairs, but my son's mother and I had a child together at a very young age. We have always maintained a good relationship, despite the short-lived childhood romance. The truth is we are now like brother and sister.

I decided to go out to lunch with my son and his mom in order to catch up. I always get more words out of my son when he is in the company of his mother, for some reason.

To be blunt, the boy is often distant in the presence of adults. Even though we've had our challenges over the years with his unique personality, I have learned to accept the boy for who he is. Whenever he decides to open up and talk, I do my best to be available to listen.

This particular visit just happened to be the first time I saw Brown Eyes, my son's mom, while she was expecting. The new addition to her family was due in a few months. I teased her about the fact that she had waited twenty years to decide to have another child. My son was excited about his new sibling. He may be distant in the presence of adults, but he always becomes playful and energetic around other kids.

After indulging in small talk, I began to get a little more serious. Before leaving to go abroad, Brown Eyes and I had tried to persuade our son to join one of the branches of the armed services. We figured it could help him change the lackadaisical attitude that had become his signature.

My son didn't want to attend college right out of high school. The reason he gave was his desire to "chill out" for six months in order to collect his thoughts and figure out where he wanted to go in life. Quite frankly, I wasn't feeling his decision, but Brown Eyes convinced me to give the boy a break. Unfortunately, these are the types of compromises you must endure when two parents are raising a child together but are no longer in a relationship.

After more than the six months had passed, Junior and his mom surprised me with some big news. It turns out that Junior had decided to go to school in order to become a pharmacist technician. Actually, he was almost finished and about to graduate. I had been traveling abroad for some time; his going to school was kept hush until my return.

Junior and his mother had smiles stretching as wide as the state of Texas, just knowing how proud I'd be that he had done something with himself. Their smiles turned to looks of confusion when they realized my expression was not a look of enthusiasm or excitement but that of puzzlement.

A million thoughts, none of them good, were running through my mind. For the first time, I realized that the deals and compromises that I had often found myself entering into as a parent had had dramatic consequences.

The first thing I had to ask Junior was, "What would make someone with two supportive parents and the potential to pursue any profession he wants go after a job that pays thirteen to sixteen dollars an hour?"

In some instances, certain trades can be a stepping-stone or foundation for securing a comfortable living, but they are very few and far between. Trades such as carpentry, plumbing, and truck driving are good examples of stepping-stones or foundations. Nevertheless, in my opinion, if a person is able to pursue a more secure and promising future, he should do so.

I found myself sitting there and talking until I was blue in the face. They just sat there and looked at me like I was the teacher from *Charlie Brown.* "Womp, womp, womp..."

After we finished lunch and went our separate ways, I replayed the conversation in my head. I actually felt horrible because there I was preaching to my son for not following rules and principles I had failed to teach him.

Through all the struggles and adversity I have been through in life, I feel that God blessed me to become financially literate. Even had I not been successful at building businesses, my financial literacy would have allowed me to choose a job or career that would maximize my options. This is where the idea of The Money Game started. The idea was not originally about building a business or seeking financial gain. The Money Game is a hands-on approach to learning various skills that improves your decision making in all aspects of financial literacy.

It took my own child to make me realize that there are millions in the YouTube and Facebook generation who could benefit from learning how to make sound decisions to secure a better financial future. I not only owe my sons and daughters for letting them down if I don't teach them what I learned about The Money Game, I also owe their sons and daughters for generations to come.

It's time to stop being taught to mind someone else's business and get on to minding our own business. Those who don't learn The Money Game will get left behind.

Note: The following is the actual e-mail correspondence between Brown Eyes and me. The creation of The Money Game and the birth of the trilogy was the result.

11/7/2011 Saud: *I keep thinking about our lunch the other day. There are so many things that are playing over and over in my head. It's difficult for me to believe that you have a hard time understanding why I am disappointed in our son's choices. I tried to make it as clear as possible, but I realize that I don't relate to these youngsters. What I say goes in one ear and out the other. Ironically, I still believe it is my fatherly duty to say it. You and I think so differently when it comes to life. I'm not sure why that is. We both know full well what doesn't work. What we did and experienced in our day no longer works today. Our son needs to get his game up...or fall by the wayside.*

11/20/2011 Brown Eyes: *Hey, Mr. Clark. Sorry for just getting back to you. I will agree that our lunch date left me with a lot to think about. I probably took most of it out of context. How are you? Our boy started his job last week, although I know you could care less (about the job that is). I thought I would keep you in the loop. We don't agree on so many things, you are correct. But I guess we only want what's best for them, but at the end of the day, it depends on what they want.*

11/21/2011 Saud : *Needless to say...I have to admit that I can't understand why you would disagree because the other ways that were explored provided no sense of security. I'll just settle on that he has a job and isn't getting into trouble, if that's something one aspires to these days. I love y'all both and whatever the situation is, I must learn to accept things the way they are. Either that or work on doing something about it.*

11/27/2011 Brown Eyes: *It's not often that our children grow up to be what or who we would like them to be. Yes, I am very grateful that he and his group of friends he hangs out with now chose to work little jobs and go to school instead of getting into trouble and going to jail. Maybe you will feel better if that were the case, for me it's not an option for him at all. I don't care if he makes two dollars an hour, he better make it work before he even thinks about robbing someone or something. These kids are nothing like us and this world is nothing like when we were growing up. We would all love to have money and be able to do as we want, but everything ain't for everybody, and sometimes trying to live like that come with a price we don't always want to pay.*

THE MONEY GAME

The Money Game is a set of principles that aim to completely change the way you think about money. You must begin by supplementing your traditional education with financial literacy.

Many people are familiar with the term "peeping game." Over the years, the term has become watered down and has begun to lose its value. I would like to believe that the term "peeping game" refers to recognizing trends, which in turn could assist you in securing your financial future (your move). There are countless moves that take place every day. Once you become financially literate and learn to play The Money Game, you will become better at the peeping game, getting on board with the next move, regardless of its size.

For the sake of simplicity, in this first book of the trilogy, I'll tone down the opportunities and moves, gradually getting into more depth as your financial intelligence grows, and you'll begin thinking like a veteran of The Money Game.

A veteran of The Money Game is someone whose focus is hiring intelligent people who have secured an academic degree. Many are the people who, despite their academic achievements, were taught to mind someone else's business. Yet, these people are good team players.

Some moves for a veteran would include designing a smartphone application, getting involved with the booming health care services industry, or purchasing foreclosed homes. I'm sure you can follow me on this.

These industry groups offer a huge potential for investors. This is the place where the growth lies in today's economy, with increasing demand. A Money Game veteran gets in on a trend at the beginning stages. Examples of this are both the health care industry and foreclosures.

Accessible Home Health Care documented on its website that, "It is estimated that The Healthcare Industry spending in 2006 was $2.2 trillion. That's approximately $7,498 for every person in the United States. This number is expected to grow to $12,782 by 2016. Health Care is undoubtedly an industry continuing to grow, even during difficult economic times."

The health care service industry is uniquely positioned do to unprecedented growth now and in the future. As stated in, The 2030 Problem, by James Knickman and Emily Snell, "The number of people aged sixty-five and older is expected to increase from thirty-five million in 2000, to seventy-one million by 2030." This increasing segment of the population will be cared for in their homes as they desire to age in a place of comfort and familiarity and home care services are provided.

In the foreclosure market, among 60 percent of people who bought property as an investment in 2010 paid cash, said Walt Molony, spokesman for the National Association of Realtors. "We discovered investors are definitely going for lower-priced properties," he added. "The median price of an investment home was $94,000 in 2010, down 10.5 percent from $105,000 in 2009." Foreclosure homes are almost 30 percent cheaper than the average price of properties not being seized by banks, according to realityTrac.

Such steep discounts mean some investors can make a profit while adding little value to the property. "There's a little bit of flipping going on, too," said Sharga. "They'll buy a property at deep, deep discounts; the investors will do some cosmetic work on it and sell it off to another investor at a lesser discount."

Such depressed prices allowed one subsection of the market to make money from the glut of cheap property without even purchasing any homes. These flippers claimed to simply transfer the property from the foreclosed homeowner to another buyer while increasing the price—sometimes by tens of thousands of dollars— in the process.

But what about the novice who's just beginning to learn The Money Game and has limited capital to start a business? There is plenty of room for this individual too. All of us can play The Money Game. All you have to do is increase your financial literacy. That's when you jump on your move. Let me give you an example of someone who was down and out as far as funds, but caught or created a move and came up playing The Money Game.

In the city where I am from, there is an individual we call Cousin James. Cousin James was the guy in the church suit, holding a bible, who we would sometimes tease because he didn't come out to play. For some reason he always seemed to be on his way to church.

I outgrew that immature behavior a long time ago. However, running into Cousin James at the bridge across the street from the zoo, standing in a busy intersection selling water, brought back pleasant childhood memories, so I smiled.

The first thing that crossed my mind was that Cousin James had either lost his mind or was on drugs. I hadn't seen or heard from him in years, so I pulled over to speak with him. I wanted to learn how he had become so down on his luck and ended up this way.

He was happy to see me, telling me that he had heard I had been off traveling the world. After the small talk, Cousin James convinced me that I shouldn't let the fact that he still wore hot suits fool me, as he had more going on for him than might be apparent.

It turned out that Cousin James was selling between one thousand to thirteen hundred bottles of water and vitamin water daily. He explained how he had been laid off from his job during the economic downturn. His unemployment benefits had run out, and his job search wasn't going well. It had gotten to the point where he was down to his last twenty bucks when survival mode kicked in.

Using his Sam's Club card, Cousin James purchased two cases of water and a bag of ice. He arranged his water bottles and the ice in an old cooler, setting up his new business venture on Thirty-Fourth and Girard. Much to his surprise, he sold the first two cases in two hours. As time went on, he sold more and more cases. Cousin James has since hired a few others to sell water for his business. He only goes to the location once a week, in order to keep track of sales volume. That day just so happened to be his on-site day.

As he explained all of this to me, I did the numbers in my head. His cost for each water bottle averages 25¢, with the vitamin water bottles costing $1. He sells the water for $1 per bottle and the vitamin water bottles for $2 each.

All I could say was, "Wow!" I know of street-corner hustlers who stand on their corners all day and night, risking their lives in numerous ways, for at best $150 to $200. These guys can get robbed, arrested, or even killed while standing on those corners. Yet, here is Cousin James, minding his own business, selling water with a daily profit close to $900. The so-called street hustlers are more often than not minding someone else's business.

A major difference between the two is Cousin James doesn't have to deal with the issues one faces when taking part in illicit street-corner activities. I've never heard of anyone going to prison or getting killed for selling water.

I shook Cousin James's hand and we went our separate ways. I left with a slight grin, thinking to myself that Cousin James was the real hustler—you do the math!

Small Talk, Big Money

If you have been paying attention to the downward spiral of the economy in the United States, or if you even have ears, I'm sure you hear the same thing I do: "It's really hard out there!" Are you one of the millions of people who are struggling during this economic downturn?

I was sitting back with a good friend by the name of Fella, just having a meeting of the minds, when a simple but very serious concern was put on the table. We wondered why so many people seem to be struggling financially. We shared countless stories of things we've done, while exploring numerous ideas and the unlimited options available to secure a financial future.

Neither of us believes that we are the sharpest knives in the drawer. So just what was it about Fella that made me so receptive to his ideas and him to mine? We weren't speaking naively in terms of unattainable hoop dreams. We traded thoughts about real-life options that people such as he and I can employ.

Even though we're from different states, we each came from the poor inner city, with underprivileged backgrounds. The fifth grade was the last I completed of my formal education (later going on to obtain a General Education Degree, also known as the GED); he graduated at the top of his class, excelling in academics.

Let's back up a minute and take a look at something very interesting. How could one guy be educated, the other not, yet each figures out ways to play in the Money Game with winning approaches? What do Fella and S.S. Clark have in common that makes them capable of doing what the others choose not to? How did either of them learn to play the Money Game? Despite the differences in their formal educations, they share one of the most important common denominators in securing a financial future: S.S. Clark and Fella are financially literate, a necessity in order to succeed in The Money Game. Financial literacy is a power move. You cannot continue to miss this move.

There are two sides to The Money Game. One is where the haves work less and make more. The other is where the have-nots work more while simply trying to maintain what they have.

The Money Game is for those who have the courage to pursue a financial education, not just to secure more, but to ultimately work less while making more. Make no mistake about it, you can become finically literate and successful if you apply yourself and pursue some of the concepts The Money Game introduces you to. In addition to your success, you will become motivated to teach the principles of financial literacy to both your children and their children.

However, before any of this can happen, most people need to wake up! There is a time for everything. The time for action is now! Don't miss the move. S.S. Clark is inviting people from all walks of life into The Money Game. I strongly believe that my ability to share the concepts many have learned from playing The Money Game will positively transform the future of countless individuals, especially inner-city residents. They are the ones who keep missing the moves—"the move" that was not designed for them to be a part of.

I know by now you are asking yourself, just what is "the move?" That's a great question. The move is your opportunity to get involved in something that will dramatically increase your financial well-being, such as the stock market, the dot-com bubble, the real estate boom, or the gold rush. Once the financially uninformed investor realizes that a move is taking place, The Money Game veterans have already secured their profits and begun to search for the next move.

The move is designed for a select group. It has nothing to do with race, gender, sexual preferences, or religious beliefs. It has everything to do with financial literacy and the ability to "mind your business."

Once you make the intelligent choice to improve your financial education, deciding to take control of your financial well-being like Fella, myself, and countless others, the results will speak for themselves. At the same time, all the misconceptions separating those who waste time minding others' businesses will reflect their futility.

The purpose of this book is to open your mind and give you insight on how to play The Money Game. Just as importantly, this book will start you on a path to financial independence.

Contrary to popular belief, you don't have to get the best grades in school or be the smartest kid on the block to play The Money Game well. In fact, many millionaires in the United States never attended college, and many never even graduated from high school.

What does that tell you? It means that just about anybody in this country has the potential to reach their financial goals—even if that goal is as big as becoming filthy rich! The only thing standing in our way is ourselves and the excuses we make:

"Working is all I know."

"I grew up poor."

"I don't have enough money to start my own business."

"I have a felony on my record, so I can't get a good job."

The list goes on.

If I had a penny for every excuse I've heard, I'd probably have an extra million dollars right now. But you know what they say about excuses…everyone has them and they all stink!

If you want to play The Money Game, it can happen for you regardless of your past mistakes or your present circumstance. If you doubt this, just think of Tyler Perry. He went from being homeless and sleeping in his car to starring in and producing his own plays, movies, and television sitcoms. Oh, and he made a few hundred million in the process. Remember Tim Allen, the guy from the hit TV sitcom *Home Improvement*? What if I told you that he spent several years in federal prison? I'm sure that we can all agree that he turned his life around and went on to become a very successful actor/comedian.

Charles "Roc" Dutton spent several years in a Maryland penitentiary and then went on to get major roles in successful television series and movies. Bob Johnson went from scrubbing toilets and horses' stables to founding Black Entertainment Television (BET) and later selling the media network for billions of dollars.

Have you ever read a book or seen a movie from the *Harry Potter* series? This incredibly successful series was started by a single mother who worked as a waitress and wrote books in her spare time. Not only are the books international best sellers, but by selling the movie rights to her stories the author has made untold millions. Not bad for a single mom!

But here's the truth. If you are going to reach your financial dreams, the first thing you must do is change the way you think about money. This book will help you do just that. I'm going to give you some insight into ways of thinking that will contradict conventional wisdom and even traditional education. I'm talking about knowledge that has made millionaires out of people just like you and me.

Even if the only examples you've ever known are regular Joes living paycheck to paycheck, barely making ends meet, it doesn't matter. This book will show you a new way. I'm going to help you change your way of thinking so that you can play The Money Game and increase you financial awareness and start down the road to success.

CHAPTER ONE

TRADITIONAL EDUCATION

Let's face it; we all want to be financially secure. And if you don't want to be, then maybe you are reading the wrong book. But the real problem is that most of us don't, or won't, do what it takes to achieve our financial dreams. Yet, believe it or not, in most cases it's not totally our fault.

Most of us have been miseducated by the US school system and its traditional ways of teaching. From grammar school all the way up through college, we are taught everything from English composition to advanced algebra. But the most vital skill that all of us need—the one that will determine the direction and outcome of our entire lives—is the one that the American school system fails to teach: how actual money works.

Now let me clear something up here, lest you think I am an anti-academic. I am in no way, shape, or form telling you that school is not important or that a traditional education is not beneficial. I firmly believe that school establishes our basic foundation. But once that foundation is built we must grow from there.

Think about it. In grade school we first learn colors, shapes, and the alphabet. Then we learn to read, write words, and form sentences. This pattern continues with each grade. It's a system built on progressing to the next level of English, social studies, and math, from the level taught the previous year. This continues throughout middle school and high school.

Some find this system of learning redundant and unfulfilling. Many students eventually lose interest in school. To them, the thought of finishing high school under such a mundane structure, then having to complete two, four, or in some cases six years of college is overwhelming.

From our very first day of kindergarten, we are only given an academic education. But what we also need is a financial education. How many checks did you learn to write in school? Did you have a class on how to open a savings or checking account, or how to balance a checkbook? Have you ever seen a financial statement or even know what one is? Do you know the difference between an asset and a liability? Could you name three of each? Its okay if you can't, but let me help you a second.

Here are three assets:

1. An income-producing property, such as a multifamily unit
2. A profitable business from which you draw a regular salary
3. Stocks that pay you dividends

Now here are three of the most common liabilities:

1. Your car or truck, if you don't own it outright
2. Your credit cards (when you are only making the minimum payments)
3. Your mortgage payment

If you don't understand all these terms now, don't worry. I will break down everything in layman's terms and explain how this knowledge can help you to secure your financial freedom.

I do believe you need to attend school to receive the academic learning that is paramount to a professional education, if that's your goal. The thing is, while professions such as doctor, lawyer, and accountant may earn you a decent income, how many of us actually want the stress that accompanies that type of life? And even though these professionals work extremely hard, a lot of them never get rich. With all those years of hard work you might assume a person would automatically be set financially for life, right? Absolutely not!

This may surprise you, but many professionals struggle with their finances just like everyone else. Being proficient in academics doesn't automatically qualify one to be financially literate. You would be surprised at the number of doctors and lawyers who live paycheck to paycheck.

But here's the good news: while you do have to obtain a degree to pursue a career as a lawyer or a doctor, you *do not* have to attend school to become financially secure or start your own business. I repeat: you can become financially secure without graduating from school.

History is full of individuals who achieved great financial success without completing their formal education: Thomas Edison, the founder of General Electric; Mark Zuckerberg, builder of Facebook; and Steve Jobs, mastermind of Apple Computers and the iPhone; even the world-famous Walt Disney, orchestrator of classic animation and theme parks. And there are many more in all professions—from music moguls and movie producers, to authors and club owners, who never graduated from school.

Whether it was intentional or not, we don't know. But what we do know is that all these accomplished individuals achieved their financial success through financial literacy, which means they understood how The Money Game works.

Money doesn't care if you are old, young, black, or white. It doesn't care if you are good-looking or as ugly as Steve Tyler or Biggie Smalls. Money only does what it is told to do. It just follows orders. Anybody's orders!

Money is just an idea that is used as a medium of exchange. It could be anything. For example, have you ever seen a prison movie where the inmates traded cigarettes for services? They were enjoying the barter system, with the cigarettes serving as the currency (medium of exchange).

Money is an entertainer. If you don't make it perform for you, it will perform for somebody else. Money cannot think; that's why you have to do the thinking for it.

It's only natural for most of us to have the same beliefs about money that our parents or guardians had. Those beliefs were learned by watching and listening to what they said, and more importantly, to what they did. As a result, we have learned the same spending and savings habits as our parents, who learned them from their parents, and so on.

But let me ask you this: How many of our parents are wealthy? And I don't just mean comfortable. I mean wealthy in the same way we aspire to be some day. How about your friends' parents? Probably none of them have great wealth. It's not like they didn't work hard and try. It's just that they weren't taught The Money Game and the importance of a solid financial education.

Many book-smart people think financial literacy means:

1. Go to school to get good grades.
2. Use the schooling and good grades to get a good job.
3. Work really hard and maybe you'll get a raise at your job.
4. Save money and get out of debt.
5. Your house is an asset.
6. Strive to live below your means.

Without realizing it, these deep-rooted beliefs are the major obstacles that stop most people from ever achieving true financial independence. When it comes to money, people are trained rather than educated. You train dogs to do things—respond a certain way to simple commands—but you don't educate them.

The Money Game has been around forever, but only a few took the initiative to learn the techniques needed to secure their financial freedom. Nowadays, some schools even say they offer financial education. But in all actuality its financial training they are offering, with an emphasis on saving money, which is a joke, as we will learn later in this book.

The majority of our traditional education is acquired through books. Even though some have been updated, these books have been around for decades and contain the same basic information as when they were originally written. In other words, the teachings are outdated. Schools are evolving too slowly to keep pace with our rapidly changing world, a world whose face changes almost daily thanks to advances in technology. Just think of how different the world was before Facebook and the iPhone! Just because you were an A student yesterday doesn't mean you know much today. Our old ways of thinking are so deeply embedded in us we don't realize we need to reduce our arrogance and be willing to learn new things.

Simply put, it's unlikely one will ever achieve true wealth without a proper financial education.

CHAPTER TWO

CHANGE YOUR MIND

Leaving your comfort zone and playing The Money Game can be one of the most intimidating things you'll ever have to do. But your financial future and success may very well depend on it.

Do you know the definition of insanity? It is when we consistently repeat the same behavior patterns but expect a different result each time. If you remain trapped in the same old way of thinking, you will undoubtedly follow the same old rules.

Here is why the traditional way of thinking won't work for what we are trying to do, which is achieve wealth and prosperity: Let's say you get good grades in school. As a matter of fact, you have some of the highest scores in your class. You go on to college and get a degree in the career path of your choice. Immediately after graduation—which means four years of hard work, financial struggle, and dedication to getting the job you want—you are hired at a well-paying job. You work hard, put in a lot of overtime, raise your pay scale, and decide to get a nice car to go along with the nice house you got at a steal for $300,000. You figure, why not, you have a well-paying, secure job, right?

Now let me snap you out of Wonderland, Alice. What happens if the business you work for gets into financial trouble? How about if the economy begins to get a little unstable as is the case these days and your company is forced to downsize and you are on the list? Or what if you are just laid off because your company has found a way for a computer program to replace your position for a fraction of what the company was paying you? What happens to your security then?

If you want real security, you might want to try going to jail. They have all the security you need: bars, cells, razor-wire fences, and correctional officers on standby 24/7. All jokes aside, if your "secure job" was snatched out from under you, what would you do? What would you fall back on? How would you pay for that nice house and expensive car?

Did you learn any other (nontraditional) ways to make money in school? School doesn't teach you how to play The Money Game; it teaches you the skills you need to work for someone else's company—and mind their business. The company makes the big profits, while you get a salary that is a small percentage of what the company actually earns from your labor.

Did you catch that? Minding someone else's business means working hard to ensure that someone else achieves financial success. The Money Game will teach you how to mind your own business, which will allow you to work less, while creating more assets.

Again, please don't think I'm saying not to go to school, because that's not it at all. I believe going to school and receiving a good education is vital to living a productive life. But we need to also make sure we get the proper financial education, which is usually learned from real-life, firsthand experience and (more often than not) trial and error.

By the time we do decide we want to know what's going on with our finances, we are so far behind it seems easier to keep minding someone else's business and settling for less—satisfied with nothing. We all know people who have given up on their financial dreams.

Financial success is a far-fetched dream to a lot of people because it isn't handed to them on a silver platter. I've learned from experience that when you begin to think differently, that dream isn't so far-fetched anymore. I grew up around a lot of people who come from the projects or from poverty-stricken neighborhoods. So it should come as no surprise to find out that many of my acquaintances have a keen sense of street smarts as opposed to book smarts.

Although I believe book smarts are important to some degree, I know firsthand that a person with street smarts has the potential to excel and be far more successful than the average person who did well and got good grades in school.

The thing that separates book smarts from street smarts is real-life experience. I have personally made, and been involved with making, an extremely large amount of money using street smarts. I have also watched all that money get spent nearly twice as fast as it was made. The problem is I didn't understand The Money Game and what to do with the money once it was in my possession. You wouldn't believe how many times I've heard some of my closest associates say they wish they knew then what they know now. But even if all that money was still standing on the table, a shift in our way of thinking would have to occur in order to have it grow and help us achieve the lifestyle that so many of us dream about.

They say money cannot buy happiness. I say we should all have the opportunity to see for ourselves! Let's get it together, or forget it forever. Everybody's future starts today. The Money Game awaits!

CHAPTER THREE

CHEATERS ALWAYS WIN

How many of us had a subject in school that we thought was a little challenging—something we really struggled with? Do you remember no matter how hard you tried, or how many hours you studied, you still had a subject that you just couldn't figure out? What happened when it came time for the big test? You were so nervous that you may not have been able to finish the test.

If you took a peek at someone else's test (or even daydreamed about taking a peek) you'd better wake up and apologize, and you still might be given a failing grade. Why? Because we are taught that if we receive help from someone else it is considered cheating. But in the real world "cheating" happens every day, and it is considered the smartest thing to do. And in actuality, it is the thing that makes the most sense.

Look at a big law firm that takes on a large-scale corporate case. There are countless paralegals and attorneys all working on a single project—all sharing relevant information with each other.

Look at doctors or nurses in a hospital. A lot of times there are symptoms that are unfamiliar to the physician in charge, and he or she has to consult with another physician to confirm the diagnoses. Then they collectively come to a conclusion on what the best treatment will be for the patient. In real life this is called help. But in school it would be considered cheating.

I don't know about you, but if I'm in a hospital with any kind of illness that my regular doctor can't diagnose or doesn't know how to treat, I most certainly hope he would consult with another physician with expertise in that area.

Question: Are you good at math? In school, math was one of my favorite subjects. I was always very proud of myself when I scored a 90 or 95 percent on a math test. But I noticed that a lot of people struggled in this area. I met my former girlfriend Puckels by sharing an answer on my math test while in school. Whenever I had to show Puckels how to do a math equation, or how to solve a problem, I confused myself if I tried to do it using the math books. You spend so much time focusing on how to remember the formulas you forget what you are applying it to!

The easiest way for me to learn and to show others how they can solve problems is by using real-life examples. If you give a child three one-dollar bills, take him to an ice cream shop, and let him buy all the ice cream cones he can with that money, he will remember the experience and look forward to doing it again. But if the next week you go to the same ice cream shop, hand the kid three one-dollar bills, then take away two of them—so instead of buying three ice cream cones the child can buy only one—that child will be anxious to know what happened to the rest of the money.

You will be amazed at how whatever explanation you give the child about how that money was subtracted from the whole amount and now equals whatever is left will be learned in a matter of minutes.

In school, you can try to teach children basic addition and subtraction for years and sometimes they still won't be able to grasp what you are trying to show through books. But try to teach the same lessons using treats or toys and the child will pick it up immediately.

Adults are the same way. If you want to teach an adult, the most effective way is to use real-life examples of something that's important to them.

Have you ever noticed how people get really intelligent and business-minded right around tax return time? They sit up straight, adjust their posture, and pay close attention to what the accountant (or whoever is filing their taxes) has to say about their finances and future income. Why do you think that is? If we applied the same attention to raising our awareness of how The Money Game really works, by establishing our financial education, many of us would be in a much better financial position today.

With all our advancements in technology, nearly half of the United States population has a smart phone. It places the internet at our fingertips. It has become easier to generate cash flow. The problem is that we are not taught how to actually make money. Instead we are taught to work hard and mind someone else's business so that person can make even more money off our labor! I'm not saying working for someone else is wrong. I am saying that not knowing how to invest the money that you make working for someone else is very wrong.

Everyone knows Bill Gates to be a computer genius. Did you also know that Ole Billy is actually a financial genius? He knows how to make money. And not with book smarts. His focus was on building his corporation, so he hired the smartest guys in their class to mind his business.

Mr. Gates didn't create his Microsoft programs himself. He purchased the technology of somebody who was a computer genius and created a business that generated a lot of cash flow from the technology he purchased.

Mr. Gates chose to change his way of thinking, which allowed him to work smart. That's the primary mentality that wealthy people possess and poor people do not. They let their money work for them, instead of them working for their money. They have a good understanding of The Money Game.

The way Bill Gates became rich is a classic example of what the traditional school system would consider cheating and also happens to be the way most large businesses and corporations have amassed their fortunes. The school system's view of how Microsoft cheated is by allowing someone else to do the work (invent software and computer applications) and then Mr. Gates buying that work (like buying test answers) and turning it into huge profits. Whose fault is it that the technology inventors didn't have the financial education that Bill Gates had? If they would have been taught The Money Game in school, instead of just academics, they would have a lot more wealth to go along with all those book smarts of theirs.

CHAPTER FOUR

HOW YOU THINK IS EVERYTHING

There are a lot of people who think that starting, running, or owning a business is extremely complicated, or is some totally different world than that of a street hustler. I tell you from firsthand experience on both sides of the spectrum, it's not. In fact, the two seemingly different worlds couldn't be more alike. The only difference is the terminology.

As I've mentioned, I know many people with street smarts who believe you need a high IQ to play The Money Game and be successful in a business or corporate environment. What turns off most of these people are unfamiliar words. But the crazy thing is we all know what those words mean, we just have a different terminology or slang.

Let me give you a simple example: the word "consignment." In the retail industry that's an everyday word. It's also an everyday word in the street industry. It just has a different name. Most street hustlers refer to it as being "fronted."

Let's look at the *Webster's Dictionary* definition:

Consignment—a shipment of goods sent to a dealer for sale with payment due after the sale of the goods.

Can you see how *Webster's* definition is so similar to the street industry's slang term of "being fronted"?

Another word commonly used in the retail industry is "factor." *Webster's* definition:

Factor—one who transacts business for another. In the streets, a factor is known as a middleman.

For example, let's say you want to open a clothing store. You have a building ready to be leased, but you need some inventory (clothing). You could go to the Magic Show to find inventory. The Magic Show is an annual convention held in Las Vegas that has hundreds of apparel vendors showcasing their merchandise to the public. The vendors include big names from Sean John, True Religion, Rock and Republic, all the way down to the newest upstart—clothing companies looking to make a name for themselves.

You name the company, and believe me they will have a kiosk or some type of setup at the convention. Once you find some vendors you like, you would contact a factor to pay the vendors. You would work out a payment schedule to pay back the factor for whatever was purchased, plus any additional interest that the factor charges. A factor works as a broker in order to bridge the two sides for a transaction. Only licensed brokers are authorized to make direct purchases from the distributing vendor.

Once you start to learn the language and familiarize yourself with certain common terms, doing legitimate business is a lot easier than you might think.

Two of the most important words you need to master are "asset" and "liability." Let's look at the technical definition from *Webster's*:

Asset—anything owned that has value; the accounting entries showing the resources of a person or business (holding, possessions, and capital).

Liability—a debt of a person or business; something that works to one's disadvantage (obligation, indebtedness, answerability).

In layman's terms, and for your goal of creating wealth, an asset is anything that brings in money or puts profits into your pockets or your business account. On the other hand, a liability is anything that takes money out of your pocket or business account. Learn these two words and understand their meanings because they are the basics of building wealth or creating debt.

Once we train ourselves to look at all purchases as either assets or liabilities we will begin to take control of our financial condition. The majority of us were raised or taught to focus on income in order to live well and get the things we want in life. But our focus should be on acquiring assets that will ultimately produce income. Remember when I said that we have to change the way we think about money, and that new way of thinking will often contradict conventional wisdom? Well, what you think about this statement: paper money is *not* real.

That's right! The same stuff you use to go into the corner store to buy your four wings and fries or use at Justin's and Houston's to pay for the surf and turf is not real.

Hold on, don't let me lose you. Everything will become clear in a minute.

CHAPTER FIVE

THE TRUTH ABOUT MONEY

Let me ask you a simple but crazy question: Do you know what money actually is? When I mention money, what is the first thing that comes to mind? Green pieces of paper decorated with faces of dead presidents, right? Well guess what: those of us who think that way about money are on the outside looking in.

Here's the technical definition of money:

Money—stamped pieces of metal; any paper notes authorized by the government as a medium of exchange.

Now let me put that in layman's terms. The government prints trillions of little green pieces of paper (called promissory notes) that are supposed to take the place or represent the real money (the stamped pieces of metal).

I'm not a big history buff, but when it comes to The Money Game I want to know what's going on. Here's an important piece of history about money that everyone needs to know. In 1971, President Nixon took the United States dollar off the gold standard and changed the rules of money. This was a dramatic shift. Overnight, savers of money became losers.

Most of us are sleeping with our eyes open. So let me wake you up real quick. Pay close attention to these words: *paper money is not real.*

Someone once said, "Money is the root of all evil." But that's not true. Where I come from, *not* having money is the root of all evil.

There's nothing funny about being broke. I have witnessed, and been asked to get involved in, some crazy things to improve my financial situation. I know people who to this day live by the motto "I'll get this money by hook or crook." One way or another. And, unfortunately, most of the time it's the other. You know what I'm talking about.

It's not the money that brings the problem; it's the lack of it. Think about the recent downward spiral in the economy. With layoffs, foreclosures, and unemployment reaching record levels, people have been doing all types of things to support themselves: robbing, stealing, and selling off all the comforts and goods they can in order to survive. You name it and it's been done.

But once again, money is not the cause of these problems. A lack of money is. That lack of money exists mainly because we are not taught the basics of The Money Game—how to generate it (legally) and most importantly how to keep the money you make and have it earn even more money for you.

It's relatively easy to make money. But if you don't know what to do with it it's very hard to keep. We have all made some money at some point in our lives—whether legally or illegally. But where is that money now? Did you spend it on an asset or a liability? More than likely, if you don't have it now or can't account for it, then it was wasted on liabilities.

Don't worry; all of us have done the same thing. Many people don't want to accept the truth about money. They refuse to accept that there are only two sides to this story. There's the falsehood they choose to believe, because it's what they really want to hear. And there's the truth, as crazy as it might sound: those little pieces of green paper with dead men's faces on them are not real.

There is good news, though. That unreal money does allow us to buy or gain control of very real assets. Did you know that most rich people do not work for their money? That is not a misprint, so you can read it again, but you read it right the first time. Most rich people don't work for money. Only the poor, those who don't understand The Money Game, do.

Now when I say rich and poor, I am not speaking in terms of a person with a mansion on MTV *Cribs* versus someone living in a subsidized housing project. I'm speaking in terms of how you *think*. Rich people work to build, create, or acquire assets that produce income. That income then works for the rich to make them even richer. They mind their own business!

Have you ever actually observed any rich people? They don't seem to ever work hard, do they? In fact, it seems poor people work two to three times harder than rich people. We have to realize that the key to real wealth is not how hard you work, but how smart you work. Working smarter, not harder, is one of the core principles of The Money Game.

And I don't mean academically smart, but rather financially smart. A poor person will work extremely hard to earn a pay raise, or put in many overtime hours to earn some extra income. A rich person's work consists of finding different vehicles (routes to a certain goal) to finance (purchase) assets and create income streams that will yield (produce) profits for generations to come. In other words, while poor people are struggling to make it from one week to the next on a measly salary, rich people are creating future wealth for themselves, their children, and their children's children.

How many times have you heard someone say, "It's rough out here," "Times are hard," and "Things are not like they used to be"? Next time you hear that, tell the person to toughen up and stop complaining because The Money Game awaits.

So many people want things to go back to how they used to be or they dwell on the times when it wasn't so hard out in society. Who doesn't want a change for the better? The problem is that nobody wants to do anything to bring real change, but everybody wants to reap the benefits. I have a strong belief that we do what we have to do, so we can do what we want to do. It's simple.

Do you like nice clothes? How about expensive cars? Would you like to have enough money to travel to different parts of the world? Or how about just sleeping like a baby at night because you don't have to worry about how your bills will get paid? If you are willing to learn The Money Game and change the way you think, I guarantee that you can live any way that you desire. The hardest part is understanding that the employee mindset you've been taught doesn't work, and will never gain you true financial independence.

The more you increase your financial intelligence, the more money you will make and the more financially secure you will become. Financial intelligence is simply knowing how money works and how to create more of it. I've encountered individuals who make their money in the streets (through illicit means) actually very financially intelligent. They have life experience and have mastered the art of turning very little into something substantial. The problem is they have taken their energy and ability to make money and used it in the wrong environment.

Let's look at a hypothetical situation. Say we have a man named Sole who couldn't get the job he wanted because he had a felony on his record. Or maybe he was downsized from his place of employment. Sole filled out countless applications and went on numerous interviews, but never was hired. Finally, frustrated with his attempts to find employment, Sole turned to illicit activities.

Without enough money to start off on his own, Sole decided to get "fronted" a package from a local street dealer. The bill on the package was $800. After two days of utilizing his salesman abilities, the bill was paid and Sole had an additional $450 in his pocket.

Sole decided it wasn't such a bad experience, so the next day he repeated the same transaction. This went on for several months. Because of his traditional way of thinking and not understanding the principles of The Money Game, Sole saved all his profits for those few months, keeping the money in a safe hidden in his cousin's basement. In Sole's mind, he was ahead of the game.

For a while everything went smoothly. But the easy money and fast profits were permanently interrupted when Sole was arrested.

And to his great dismay, the entire $17,500 he had accumulated had to be used for bail and attorney fees.

Back to square one. If Sole had been taught The Money Game could he have ended up in a much different financial situation? Yes!

Too bad Sole never read this book!

CHAPTER SIX

MAKE YOUR HUSTLE YOUR BUSINESS

I will never promote or advocate living the "street life" because I know firsthand the dangers and consequences that come along with the illusion of easy money. What I am offering is an opportunity for you to learn The Money Game and invest for your future. So regardless of how bad the economy gets you won't have to resort to government entitlements or any type of criminal activity.

Using the example from the previous chapter, let's look at what our friend Sole could have done with his money. You may recall that he saved all his profits (which did take a lot of discipline), but he stashed the money in a dark safe where it couldn't grow.

Another core principle of The Money Game is money must continue to work in order for it to grow. Stagnant dollars will eventually lose value.

The first thing Sole should have thought about was how many assets he could have acquired with his profits. Remember, assets are anything that brings money *in*.

What if Sole went to a car auction and purchased a decent vehicle for $1,000 to $1,500? And what if he had some minor work done on the car—tune up, oil and brake job, plus wash and wax detailing—for an additional $200? Typically, cars bought at an auction for this amount resell to the public for about $3,000 to $3,500. On the low end of your investment, you make $1,300; on the high end $1,800. And it's all legal.

In no way do I endorse or condone the way that Sole accumulated his funds. The basis of The Money Game is financial literacy so that's the focus, not the person's livelihood. It's sad how the lower class seem to be the ones who are judged and frowned upon for the choices they make. Needless to say, the very same rules are held in a completely different regard when compared to a previous United States president whose father was a well-known bootlegger.

What if you sold two cars a month? How about three or four? With the time, energy, and work ethic I see in people who put fifty, sixty, or seventy hours per week trying to get a fat overtime paycheck, I don't see a problem.

Let's take another quick glance at the numbers. For our profit margin, we'll use the middle between the low end and the high end. Selling two cars a month for a profit of $1,550 each earns $3,100, which is $37,200 a year. Four cars would increase your income to $6,200 per month and a pretty decent $74,400 a year. These are just ballpark figures, but I think you can see the potential here.

Or maybe you want to get involved in fashion. You like clothes, shoes, and apparel, and want to make your money that way. You could simply go downtown, or to the nearest clerk's office, and file for a vendor's license that would allow you to buy and sell certain goods to the public.

Clothing has huge potential to be a good source of revenue simply because of the markup and the profit margin that can be made on each piece. With the Internet and wholesale dealers, you'll discover that there's a lot of money to be made.

How many assets do you have? How many liabilities? If you have more liabilities than assets you will never become financially secure. The key to a prosperous life full of secured wealth is very simple: have more assets than liabilities. That means always having more coming in than going out.

You probably think this is easier said than done. But I'm sure there are many potential assets available to you right now. I say "potential assets" because some things can actually be an asset or liability depending on how you think.

I know a lot of people who believe their home is an asset because they pay mortgage on it and have equity in it. The problem is that your home mortgage must be paid each and every month, which means a constant stream of money *going out* every thirty days. This is a classic liability.

If you can't find a way to pay the mortgage, you risk losing your home and any equity you have in it. I'm not saying a home is not a good investment because in many cases it can be. I'm saying that the way you make your home a good investment is by having an asset pay for it.

Here's an example of your home being paid for by an asset. Say you purchase a four-unit, multifamily home and decide to live in one of the units. Let's suppose your mortgage payment on the property is $2,400. You receive $825 in rent from each of the other three apartments. Out of the $2,475 that comes in from rent, you pay your mortgage and look for something else to eventually invest the extra $75 into. Now your home is an asset because not only do you not have money going out, you have your mortgage being paid, equity building in the property, and additional money coming in. The financially intelligent way of thinking is how can I have assets pay any and all of my bills?

Can you think of any way to have extra money coming in each month? If you like handbags or accessories you could buy a few bags and other items wholesale and resell them to the public for a nice profit. You could sell them at work, in the salon or barbershop, at the carwash, or online. You could sell them to your family, your friends, and your friends' friends. The more creative you are with your marketing and sales strategies, the bigger profit you will make.

Let's say you are interested in buying a new laptop computer. You do some research online and find out that the refurbished laptops are practically new and sell for less than half the price of a new one. And they even come with a limited warranty.

The brand-new laptop you want is priced at $399, but the refurbished ones offered by a company specializing in second-hand merchandise sell for $175. You could purchase two refurbished computers for $350 and resell one for $300 to a coworker who also wants a laptop. Now you have your $400 laptop for only $50! Think in terms of how you can have what you want without having to pay for it. Being financially literate allows you to take advantage of The Money Game principles. It is these principles that become your foundation toward financial independence.

CHAPTER SEVEN

INVEST, NEVER SAVE

I've heard a lot of people say you should live below your means so that in the future you will have something saved. But what about right now? Am I supposed to be miserable now while hoping to be secure someday in the future? Who made these crazy rules and more importantly why? It was probably somebody who had a lot of book smarts and didn't understand The Money Game.

I don't know about you, but I don't want to struggle or just survive. Not now, not later, not ever! I've struggled financially before and I hated every minute of it. The *only* people who struggle are the ones who don't fully understand how money actually works.

You can never get rich by simply saving money. This may sound crazy because of how your old way of thinking has clouded your judgment. But don't worry, eventually you will begin to think more clearly and by playing The Money Game it will become as natural as breathing. I'll also bet whoever told you that you should save money isn't rich and probably doesn't have much money at all. My son's decision to pursue a career that pays $13 to $16 dollars an hour as a pharmacy tech is a classic example.

The reason why saving will never get you rich is because of inflation. Let's go to *Webster's*:

Inflation—an increase in the amount of money and credit in relation to the supply of goods and services; an excessive, persistent increase in the general price level as a result of this, causing a decline in purchasing power.

Now in layman's terms: whatever money you have today will not be worth that same amount in the future. In other words, your money actually loses value the longer you hold it or save it. Without an understanding of what inflation is, a person won't understand that the twenty-dollar bill he has in his pocket today won't buy the exact same thing in the future. According to my grandmother, once upon a time you could buy a hot dog, chips, and a soda for ten or fifteen cents. Ten or fifteen cents! What the hell happened? I'll tell you what happened: inflation.

That ten or fifteen cents doesn't have the same value (or purchasing power) as it did in the past. How much would a hot dog, chips, and a soda cost today? Whatever answer you come up with, it'll certainly be a lot more than fifteen cents.

But what if my grandparents had just saved their fifteen cents and tried to buy something to eat with it today? My dear sweet grandparents would find themselves out of luck, and they would surely starve to death.

Let me give you another basic example. Do you remember (or know anyone who remembers) when you could go to a public payphone and put a dime in the slot and make a call? If you put a dime in the payphone now, the damn thing will probably spit the dime back at you! Or maybe you remember when the cost of a call was just a quarter. How much are those calls now?

What about when you could write a letter, or pay a bill, stick it in an envelope with a twenty two-cent stamp, and drop it in the mailbox. Try that today and the post office will stamp "Return to Sender" on the envelope and return the letter to you before you even get back from the mailbox!

Money must multiply just to keep up with inflation. In order to be ahead of the game, your money needs to multiply faster than inflation. So how on earth can saving money be a smart thing to do?

Try waltzing into a movie theatre with your girlfriend and only two dollars expecting to buy tickets. They'll probably arrest you and place you in the psych ward. After the mall cops rough you up a little bit. Whatever money you have today will *not* be worth the same amount fifteen, ten, or even five years from now. So why would you bother to save it?

Your focus should be on investing, not saving. I cannot stress this point enough. Invest, don't save. And your investments should be assets—things that generate income. I believe it to be a wise position to have some funds set aside for an emergency. I suggest four to six months of your current living expenses. With such insurance it makes it possible that you can stay afloat during an emergency. A Money Game player can breathe a little easier.

My personal favorite is real estate because of the potential income you can receive when you do your homework and purchase the right properties. But what if you don't have enough money right now to invest in real estate? Well, you'll have to start with smaller assets, like some of the ones mentioned in this book. These opportunities are everywhere if you only keep an open mind, peep some game, and begin to look.

Remember, assets are anything with value, or for our purposes anything you can buy and make a profit from. This is where uncommon sense comes into play. The majority of people are stuck in the dinosaur age of saving money and not investing. But with a financial education and some uncommon sense, we can begin to think differently and build wealth playing the Money Game.

Let's look at a few assets that you can acquire for a relatively small amount of money. A few examples would be flat-screen TVs bought at a wholesale discount, clothing bought at a vendor discount, car rims, pool tables, adult novelty items, twelve to fifteen passenger vans, laptop computers, lawn mowers, and the list goes on.

Just about any tangible product—depending on how you see it—can be used as an asset. If the product can be purchased below cost and resold with a profit, it can be placed in your asset column.

If the item or product is something that can be used more than once or something that can generate a continuous stream of income, it would be considered one of your more important assets.

Let's look at a few liabilities: mortgage, car note, phone bills, cell phone bill, credit card bill, college loans, debts, daycare fees, and anything else that you use your hard-earned cash to pay for. Our goal should be to have as many assets as we have liabilities. If we manage to accumulate assets that create or produce income that pays for all of our liabilities and still have additional income left over (possibly to invest in more assets) we are playing The Money Game and experiencing true wealth.

What steps or direction do we take to begin our journey toward accumulating true wealth? Well, that's up to each individual and their particular interest. I would suggest that you find something you like and find it below cost. Or pick something you truly enjoy doing and devise a plan to generate some type of income or fee from doing it. That will begin your transition into playing The Money Game.

CHAPTER EIGHT

MASTER YOUR CREDIT

Your credit history could be one of the most important factors in determining whether or not you achieve wealth. You know the saying "you never get a second chance to make a first impression." This is oftentimes true with your credit score.

Think of banks, loan officers, credit card issuers, and any other type of organization that is able to give or loan money as an actual person. And let's call this person "Money Mike." Now, think of your credit score as another person, and let's call him "Low Key."

Money Mike is able to run his business and produce a lot of income by loaning money to people and getting that money back with interest. Money Mike has generated a lot of income with loan transactions—some good, some bad—but the way he stays in business and is able to enjoy the good life is to make good transactions. Money Mike is always looking for new people to do business with.

Money Mike usually loans money to people based on what his three buddies tell him. His buddies are always checking up and keeping tabs on everybody in town.

This is where Low Key (your credit score) comes into play. If the word on the street is that Low Key borrows money and doesn't pay it back, Money Mike won't want to do business with him. Now, if everyone is saying that Low Key is a good guy and talking about how he always borrows money and pays it back on time (with interest) he is somebody Money Mike wants to meet.

People who play The Money Game use credit and other people's money to buy assets that pay back the money they borrowed plus interest and put money into their pockets. So for them, the more they borrow, the richer they become. This is called managing your credit or debt.

Good debt is exactly the type of debt we should focus on. It allows us to purchase income-producing assets. Bad debt is anything that we borrow that won't give us a return on what we borrowed. Basically, bad debt is borrowing money for liabilities. If you're going to be in a position to be able to borrow money for assets, you need to make sure your credit score is in order and accurate.

First, let's make sure we know what the basic makeup of credit is. If you've ever applied for any sort of credit—credit card, cellular phone service, or utility service (gas, electric, water, etc.)—then you have a credit history, a credit report, and a credit score. This happened whether you knew it or not.

So why didn't somebody notify you or tell you what was going on? Well, my friend, it doesn't work that way. Do you remember when you went out and applied for your first loan or credit card? They made you fill out an application, right? What actually happened was the credit issuer called a credit bureau to check up on you.

The lender probably called one of the country's big three credit bureaus: Trans Union, Equifax, or Experian. When that bureau recognized that it didn't have any information on you, they started a credit file. The other bureaus learned about you shortly thereafter.

Say your first application was filled out for a credit card. You read it and signed the form, bought a few items, and once the bill came in you paid it. Your credit card company closely monitored the way you handled that transaction and sent every detail of what you did to all three credit bureaus. They gave the bureaus information about whether you paid on time, what percentage of the outstanding debt you paid, and whether or not you stayed within your credit limit.

The next thing you know you had a great credit history. Granted, it wasn't very deep or detailed. But guess what? It existed, and every time you paid a bill (or failed to pay) it was added to your credit file. As you accumulated more and more creditors, your file and credit report (the written version of that file) continued to grow.

Over the years, some of that information eventually falls off the report. But for the most part much of it follows you around for as long as you have managed credit. In other words, as long as you have air in those precious lungs of yours.

Six months later, there was enough information in your credit file for the credit bureau to assign you something called a credit score. In layman's terms, your credit score is a translation of your credit history put into numerical form that insurers, lenders, employers, landlords, and others use as reference to make a decision about whether they want to do business with you and how much interest to charge you if you ever want to do business with them. Every time new information about you or your credit score is reported to the bureau, your credit scores changes.

Credit scores range from 350 to 800, the highest number being the best. In most cases, you will rarely see a score below 500 or more than 800. The bulk of credit scores are provided by Fair Isaac Company out of California. The Fair Isaac Company doesn't collect credit information, and it's not a credit bureau. But it does work with all three of the large credit bureaus. What Fair Isaac Company does is take the information that those bureaus collect and turn it into your credit score or FICO (Fair Isaac Company) score.

Your credit history affects just about every part of your life in some way, shapes, or form. It affects not only if you will be able to get a new credit card but how much you can borrow, what range of interest rates you will pay, whether your line of credit will be increased, whether you qualify to rent an apartment or buy a home, if you can get a cell phone, if you can get a cash advance, whether you will actually even get the credit card you were pre-approved for, how much you will pay for homeowner's and auto insurance, and a host of other things.

For the record, employers are not supposed to look at credit scores. But in a situation where you are asked to handle a draw of cash, they will look at credit reports for any signs of trouble. Would you put a person who has a bunch of bills and delinquent debts in front of your company's cash drawer filled with fifty- and hundred-dollar bills?

In the Money Game, keeping a good credit score is a tool that can do wonders for your financial future. If your credit score is more than 620, you will be able to borrow more money than those with credit scores lower than 600, who will pay very high interest rates. Plus, once you raise your score up past 700, you will be able to borrow money at the very best price and low interest rates. The higher your score the lower interest you pay to borrow money.

There really is no credit score you can have that will prevent you from getting a credit card, not even 500. If you have a very low credit score, the bank or lender will ask you to deposit some money to secure the credit card until you prove you can pay your bills. In this case, there is an eighteen- to twenty-four-month period of proving yourself before the bank or lender considers unsecuring the card. However, you will still have the credit card and be building credit; your interest rate will just be a little high for that period.

Interestingly, you can get to a point where a credit card issuer thinks your score is too high. In the credit card issuer's world, a score of 720 or 730 is ideal and 800 is too high. What sense does that make? Well, from a business standpoint, it makes a whole lot of sense. There is a correlation between credit inactivity and a very high credit score. People who use their credit card rarely—or only in the case of an emergency—represent more of a cost than a benefit to credit card companies.

People with very high credit scores rarely pay their bill late, which means the credit issuer won't be able to make much money in interest or late penalty fees. Since the credit card companies still have to send a statement once a month and literature when they make a change in any programs they offer, it actually costs the companies money to keep doing business with people that have very high credit ratings.

Nowadays many companies are encouraging the consumer to go paperless. Receiving your statement electronically is an excellent way to keep track of your paper history. I caution that setting up the transition from having your monthly statement via snail mail to e-mail can possible change your current billing cycle. A family member of mine chose the electronic option and continued to pay her bill as she normally did on the twentieth of each month. When she switched to paperless her billing cycle made her payments due on the first. She had forgotten that she even signed up for the paperless. After not receiving a bill via mail for three consecutive months, she called and discovered that her bill had come electronically. Consequently she ended up with three late payments on her credit report. I suggest that we make sure that we are on top of all affairs that can negatively affect our credit reporting.

There are a number of ways you can improve your credit score. We will go over some of them shortly. For now, let's make sure we have the basics covered. For instance, you should be consistent about using your name. Make sure it's the same last name. If you use a hyphen in your name use it all the time. If you include Jr. or II in your name, use it consistently. Say you took your maiden name as your middle name—make it legal. This is to make sure the credit bureau doesn't confuse your information with someone else's.

Let's take a look at how your score is computed. Thirty-five percent of your score is based on how well you pay your bills. Start boosting your rating by paying on time. When you make late payments your score suffers depending on how late and how frequent your delinquencies are. If you have only one thirty- or sixty-day late payment, that's much less damaging than fifteen late payments during the last five years.

There is also a lot of attention paid to how recently those delinquent payments occurred. A single incident five months ago still counts. A single incident five years ago is not that relevant. As an example, one late payment in your recent credit past could lower your score by twenty points.

Thirty percent of your score is a measure of how much credit you have available to you and out of that credit, how much you are using. It's best to use 20 to 30 percent of the credit available to you.

Ten percent is based on your search for new credit (how recently you have opened or inquired about opening new accounts). Auto- or mortgage-related inquiries that result in your score being pulled by lenders within fourteen days of each other simply tell the credit bureau that you are shopping for a car or a house and are counted as one inquiry. If you have any inquiries from over twelve months ago, they won't count at all.

You must pay close attention to when you let credit card companies pull your report. One application for a single card isn't a problem. However, multiple card inquiries are a sign that you need money and are a warning flag to the credit bureau. Generally, multiple inquiries, especially if you've had credit for only a few years, can mean a loss of up to one hundred points on your credit score.

Ten percent is the financial composition of your file (bank card, debt, and installment debt). For scoring purposes it's best to have a ratio of 60 to 70 percent bank card debt and 30 to 40 percent installment debt.

Fifteen percent is a measurement of how long you have had credit. It's good to have credit cards that are more than two years old in order to help boost your rating.

Once you've had a credit card for fifteen to twenty years it won't send your score any higher. Increasing your score will be a little more challenging if you have a bankruptcy in your credit history or a late payment of over ninety days. For the most part, if that's the case, you have to maintain and manage whatever credit you have and wait for the bankruptcy or late payments to be removed from your credit history. Negative information usually stays on your report for seven years for late payment, seven years for a debt management plan (hiring a counselor), seven years for Chapter 13 bankruptcy, and ten years for Chapter 7 bankruptcy.

Your credit score is built to predict what will happen over the next thirty-four months. That is the probability that you'll fall behind or have delinquent payments coming over the next twenty-four-month window. So generally, it makes the most sense to the lender to base decisions most heavily on your behavior over the previous twenty-four months.

The three major credit bureau scores vary depending on what information each bureau keeps in its report. As far as your number for each, the median spread is thirty-five points. To get the score from Transunion or Equifax go to www.myfico.com. A single report is $12.95. Experian sells its scores at www.experian.com, but it's just a simulator, not the actual score reported to lenders. So the $14.95 Experian charges aren't the best deal. You can get a general idea of you FICO score for free at www.eloan.com and click on the scroll-down menu labeled "free credit report" on the upper right side.

If you want to closely monitor your progress, the credit bureaus offer services that either give you unlimited access to your credit report and score or will alert you to any changes on your report. The prices for this service vary but are reasonable. Equifax charges $69.95 for a year, Experian $79.95, and Transunion $63.60.

If you are only going to use one, choose the service that will give the most complete report. This is usually based on the region where you reside. Equifax is best if you live in the south and southeast; Transunion for the north and northeast; and Experian for the west.

Here are the street addresses in case you want to contact them by mail:

Transunion, P.O. Box 390, Springfield, PA 10964-0390

Equifax, P.O. Box 740241, Atlanta, GA 30374-0241

Experian, P.O. Box 949, Allen, TX 75013

If you find information on your credit report that you disagree with or do not think is accurate you can dispute the information by mail or online. If you do it by mail, the credit bureau will send you a form to fill out. Use their form or use one of the letters I have provided in the appendix as a template.

If, after investigating your claim, the credit bureau agrees with you that the information is incorrect, it must remove the information and then send you a copy of the accurate report. If the credit bureau does not agree that the information should be removed, you should write a letter explaining your version of the events and ask the credit bureau to attach it anytime your credit report is pulled. Until that matter is settled, a creditor cannot give out information that would hurt your credit standing with potential creditors or other credit bureaus. You are entitled to one free credit report a year. If free credit reports are available in your state through the Annual Credit Report Request Service, you can request a free annual credit report by phone or mail and it will be mailed within fifteen days. However, you can receive a report immediately by using this secure websitehttps://www.annualcreditreport.com/cra/index.jspto find information on how to request a free annual credit report by phone or mail.

Sample letters you can use to dispute information on your credit report or set up a payment plan to repay debt have been provided in the appendix.

Many consumers are under the impression there is nothing that can be done to change the information on their credit reports. Thankfully, this is not true. Federal law gives you the right to have misinformation on your credit reports corrected. You are ultimately responsible for assuring that your credit reports accurately represent your behavior as a consumer.

The Fair Credit Reporting Act (FCRA) gives you the right to contact credit bureaus directly and dispute items on your credit reports. You can dispute any and all items that are inaccurate, untimely, misleading, biased, incomplete, or unverifiable (questionable items). If the bureaus cannot verify that the information on their reports is indeed correct, then those items must be deleted.

Or you can then hire a firm that's reputable in assisting you at repairing your credit. I have a family member that used a firm called Lexington Law and received some positive results. I'm sure that there are other firms who also do good work. I suggest that you do your homework when searching for an ideal firm to help you with your individual needs.

Once you fully understand how your credit works, use it to play The Money Game to your advantage; meaning, use your credit to finance or purchase all the assets you can buy. If done correctly they should pay for themselves and make you wealthier in the process.

CHAPTER NINE

BUILDING YOUR CREDIT FOUNDATION

Here's an example that can help you get on track with building your FICO rating and raising capital by having different lines of credit available to you. You can start with $100, $500, or $1,000. Of course, the more you have to begin with, the faster your limits will climb.

We'll start with $1,000 to keep a nice even number. You go to a local bank or credit union of your choice. You take $1,000 and open a savings account. Wait ten working days to make sure all of your information is in their system then go back and request a loan. Explain to the bank that you already have a savings account with them and you would like a 180-day secured loan of $1,000, using your savings as collateral.

The bank will put a freeze on your savings account, using it as collateral for your loan, and grant your request. We'll call this lending establishment "Bank A."

Now go to another bank ("Bank B") and use the $1,000 you have as a loan from Bank A to open another savings account for $1,000. Wait another ten working days then go back to request another 180-day secured loan using your savings of $1,000 as collateral.

Now, you take this $1,000 and go to a third lending institution ("Bank C") and open a checking account. This will allow you to use a checkbook to do business transactions. When your first payment is due in thirty days, say $175, you write a check to Bank A for $200 using your checking account from Bank C. Once the check clears, Bank A will unfreeze $200 from your $1,000.00 savings account that they were using as collateral.

In about ten working days your payment should be due at Bank B. Write another check for $200 to Bank B from your checking account. When this check clears, you will have a total of $400 in unfrozen savings from Banks A and B.

Withdraw the $200 from each bank and deposit the entire amount into your checking account in Bank C. Now, the $400 that was withdrawn using checks is back inside your checking account. If you continue this process, it should take five months, 150 days, to repay your two loans, not 180 days.

The purpose of paying the extra $25 a month is to pay the loan off early, which means you will pay slightly less interest over the course of the entire loan. Once you have fully repaid the loans, you will have a good credit history with your bank.

Now, request another loan from each of your bank, but this time ask for an *unsecured* loan of $1,500 or $2,000. Then, repeat the same process as before. Each time you fully repay your loans, request an increase in the next loan amount.

For example, from $2,000 you may request a loan for $3,000 or $4,000. You can do this with as many banks as you can manage. I think six banks is the ideal amount. If you can get six banks to loan you up to $5,000 each, using our example, with $1,000, you have turned $1,000 into $30,000.

Playing The Money Game with a little common sense and financial education, I'm sure you can think of a few ways to invest the $30,000 and be able to pay back the loans while increasing your wealth.

CHAPTER TEN

WATCH FOR THE HOOK

If you ask the average person the question, "What is Chex Systems?" you will get an array of responses and even some blank stares. The people who are aware have usually been painfully affected by the severe effect Chex Systems can have on a person's life. The best practice is to avoid being placed on Chex Systems' list. However, this is the real world, and we face real issues.

If you have been placed on the Chex Systems list, you have probably been faced with the harsh reality of rejection! Rejection means not being able to open a new bank account, pay for goods with checks, and enjoy the other conveniences available to basic bank account holders.

Chex Systems is a database that banks use to determine the risk factor of potential customers. Banks will report you to the system if they close your account for negative balances, or if you provide false information when opening your account. Generally, the bank will list the reason. The information can stay on the Chex Systems records for up to five years.

Some banks will allow you to open an account if proof of having paid off the balance owed to the other bank is provided. Some banks will offer you an account with higher fees, which helps to offset the bank's risk in having a customer with previous mistakes. Other banks will not allow you to be a customer as long as you are on the list.

So, you're on the list; you've been rejected by your bank of choice. Now what?

You can request a report from Chex Systems if you have been denied an account in the last sixty days. The bank that rejected you can provide, upon request, information as to how to receive a report from Chex Systems. Once you receive the report, you will need to clear up any fees you owe the other banks. When you have done this, request that the bank you have paid off send in a report that the account has been paid. Be sure to request a copy of all correspondence. This can be used as proof to the other bank.

You can avoid being reported to Chex Systems by contacting your bank if for some reason your account carries a negative balance. Some banks are willing to work with you, as long as you are making a real and steady effort to bring your account back into the positive.

It's important to remember that Chex Systems is not a bank. Chex Systems is a reporting agency that works with the banks to help identify high-risk clients.

While Chex Systems does not directly approve or deny bank accounts, if you are listed in the Chex Systems database, it is unlikely you will get a bank account of any kind at any major bank. Nearly 90 percent of all banks in the United States use Chex Systems in their account decision process.

CHAPTER ELEVEN

A HELPING HAND

"Cash, debit, or credit?" "I'm sorry; we only accept major credit cards." "You will need a major credit card to hold your deposit." Do these words sound familiar? These can be some of the most dreaded words we, as consumers, can imagine hearing, when we can't fulfill the request. If the creditors do not consider you "credit-worthy" these are the obstacles you will face.

Well, guess what? There is a way out! There is an effective approach to building your credit history, proving your credit-worthiness. Secured credit cards!

Banks will issue secured credit cards to clients who make a deposit into a savings account, money market, or certificate of deposit. The amount of the deposit varies from $250 to $500. These funds are considered your security, and will even earn a little interest, since they are being held in a savings account. Your credit limit will be equal to the amount that you deposit. It can be viewed as borrowing funds from yourself, while improving your credit in the process.

It is important to remember that a secured credit card is, in fact, a credit card, not a debit card. If full payments are not made each month, then interest is charged on the outstanding balance. Even though the card is secured, it is still possible to damage credit by not making monthly payments. The bank will only use your security deposit as a last resort to collect on unused funds.

Before you choose a bank, you should ask a few questions:

Does the bank report monthly to the three major credit bureaus?

Banks have to pay to report to the credit bureaus. So beware, some banks are cheap and neglect reporting. If they don't report, your credit rating will not improve.

How long will it take to qualify for an unsecured credit card?

The credit card company should want to keep you as a customer, so most will qualify you for an unsecured card after a period of making all your payments on time. The average period is about one year. It can take several months to see an improvement in your credit history. A good indicator is when credit card offers start coming in the mail. However, it is wise to continue to take things slowly. The successful management of the secured credit card is excellent preparation for the unsecured credit cards in the future.

Are the fees reasonable?

Fees are to be expected, but be mindful that some banks will hit you with outrageously high fees. The application fee along with annual or monthly fees should not be more than a total of $100 to $150 during the first year.

Is the security deposit flexible?

Everyone knows that higher credit card limits are better. But what if you cannot afford much for your security deposit right now? The best cards should offer some flexibility. For example, you can start with a $300 deposit for a $300 limit. But later on, when you can afford to do so, an opportunity should be given to raise the $300 limit to as high as $3,000, simply by adding more to your security deposit.

Capital One (#1 in 2010)

Some secured credit cards charge higher rates and fees. The Capital One Secured Credit Card offers you competitive terms—and as an added benefit of this card, you can track your credit with enrollment in Credit Inform, a service that provides you access to your credit score, as well as other credit tools and information.

Capital One reports your credit standing to the three major credit bureaus. Credit standing includes things like whether you make your full minimum payment on time every month. A history of good credit standing can help build your credit. Not making your minimum payments on time each month can damage your credit.

Purchase APR 22.9% variable APR

Transfer Info 22.9% variable APR; no transfer fee

Annual Fee $29

Minimum Security Deposit $49, $99, or $200 refundable deposit based on your creditworthiness

Credit Line $200–$3,000. Minimum security deposit gets you a $200 line. Deposit more to increase your line.

Applied Bank

Applied Bank, headquartered in Wilmington, Delaware, is a Delaware State Chartered Bank and an FDIC insured, Equal Housing Lender. They have been providing banking services since 1996. Applied Bank provides secured and unsecured Visa and MasterCard credit cards to people with little or no credit history.

9.99% fixed APR

First Progress Platinum

The First Progress Secured Credit Card is a full-feature Platinum MasterCard® with a credit line based on a security deposit rather than on a credit score. The card is designed to advance the accumulation of new information in a credit file by reporting account activity to all three of the major national credit bureaus every month. And because it's a full-feature Platinum MasterCard, the card provides the protection, convenience, and prestige of the worldwide MasterCard system.

As of February 29, 2012, the Annual Percentage Rate (APR) for purchases is 14.99 percent and the APR for cash advances is 19.99 percent. These APRs will vary with the market based on the prime rate. The minimum interest charge is $1.50. The cash advance fee is $10 or 3 percent of the cash advance, whichever is greater. The foreign transaction fee is 3 percent of the transaction amount.

Sign up with a minimum $300 security deposit
Variable APR for purchases and cash advances
Set credit limit between $300 and $2,000
Full-featured MasterCard protection and benefits
Low annual fee of $39

Pay your balances on time and you won't be charged any interest. However, your APR will consistently remain low even if you are unable to pay your balance in full every month.

When you sign up for the First Progress Platinum Secured, you have the option of setting your individual credit limit with a $300 minimum in your account. However, your account may not exceed the maximum limit of $2,000.

Your security deposit is insured by the FDIC and your account activity is reported on a monthly basis to all three leading US bureaus, including Experian, Transunion, and Equifax. This allows you to build your credit line and establish financial growth in due time

First Premier Bank

Annual Percentage Rate (APR) for Purchases 36.0%
    APR for Cash Advances 36.0%
    Set-up and maintenance fees: Some of these set-up and maintenance fees will be assessed before you begin using your card and will reduce the amount of credit you initially have available. Based

on your initial credit limit of $300, your initial available credit will be only about $225.

Processing Fee $95 (one-time fee)

Annual Fee $75 for first year
After that, $45 annually.

Monthly Servicing Fee None for first year (introductory) After that, $75 annually ($6.25 per month).

Transaction Fees

Cash Advance either **$6.00** or **5%** of the amount of each cash advance, whichever is greater.

Foreign Currency 3% of each transaction amount in US dollars.

Penalty Fees Up to $35.00.

Return Item Charge Up to $35.00.

Orchard Bank

The Orchard Bank Secured MasterCard is an excellent card for establishing or rebuilding credit in your name. It comes with a low 7.99 percent variable purchase APR, and the first year's annual fee will be waived.

Introductory APR and Duration N/A

Variable Purchase APR 7.99%

Variable Penalty APR 29.99%

Annual Fee $0 Introductory first year, $35 per year thereafter

Other Fees to Open Account $200 Minimum Security Deposit

CHAPTER TWELVE

FROM EMPLOYEE TO EMPLOYER

Let me ask you some serious questions: Do you like your job of minding someone else's business? Do you like your boss? Are you a dedicated worker? Do you have good people skills?

These are questions you may have been asked in reference to where your paychecks come from. But the big question should be, "Why am I minding someone else's business, using my time and talents to make them rich, when I could be minding my own business?" If you were to play The Money Game and put the same hard work and energy into your own business as you do for other people's business, you could generate a decent source of income. And that source of income would be a solid asset. And the harder you worked on your business, the greater the income and the better the asset.

Here's another question that may require some deep thought: Are you happy? I mean truly happy and living the life you want to be living? If the answer is no, then you need to ask yourself, Why not? A wise man once said, "If you always do what you've always done, then you'll always get what you've always got." You owe it to yourself (and your family) to at least try to play The Money Game and attempt to improve your happiness and financial well-being. What could it hurt? You already know what doesn't work; you might as well try to figure out what does work. And that starts with your way of thinking and how you view money.

Always remember, money doesn't think for itself. It needs you to think for it. And whatever you come up with that's what the money will do. If you don't tell money to do anything, it won't. But if you come up with a plan to make money work for you, then the money will obey and do exactly what you will it to do.

If things are a little tight for you right now, you can still play The Money Game by making the transition from employee to employer on a part-time basis. No pressure. Keep your present job, but focus on what you need to do part time to build and mind your own business.

Let's look at a few examples that may give you some ideas on how to get started. How many of us like to eat? Bingo! Found one! Look at something as simple as cooking. If you can cook, or have a favorite dish you prepare, why not sell it? Maybe you don't want to do a lot of meal preparations, or spend long hours every day getting your food to the public. In that case you can go with ready-made items.

Say you went into the food business. Where would you start? First, you would give your business a name and then incorporate the name (under LLC—Limited Liability Company, or one of the other corporate entities available). There are all sorts of websites that will walk you through the setup of your LLC step by step.

My research shows that many states have advantages and dis-advantage are the best places to incorporate your business. I'm not attempting to give you any legal advice here, so consult with an attorney or representative of business entity set up, and ask any and all questions in regards to the best way to set up your company structure.

Go to an auction and find some mobile food trucks, carts, or stands, the same stands you see hot dog vendors in on the corners of inner-city streets or downtown metropolitan areas. Next, get a food vendor license from the courthouse or municipal building that issues them. Then, go online and look for large wholesale suppliers of the type of food you want to sell or go to a local wholesale warehouse like BJ's or Sam's Club. You can find the simplest foods in bulk for very low prices at warehouses like these. I'm talking about unsophisticated foods like hot dogs, hamburgers, fries, wings, mozzarella sticks, pizza, and a bunch of other ready-made frozen goods that you can package together and sell to the public. The turnover, profit-wise, is very good.

Once you have some clientele from minding your own business, you can step things up a notch and hire someone to work your food stand so you can purchase another one and set up someplace else.

A lot of times, hospitals and basketball games already have a few stands surrounding them, which are more than likely the best food traffic spots. You can either try to find an equally visible spot and promote your business there, or look for a different venue.

Another idea is to put your food stand near a college. Ideally one with a large population and in an area with a nice climate that would allow you to stay out longer, possibly all year around. If the climate warrants, you could also sell ice cream and different frozen items in the summer. When it comes to cash flow, these types of items are underestimated, to say the least.

I know a guy in Philadelphia, let's call him Chris, who runs a hot dog stand on the corner near Children's Hospital in West Philly. This is a relatively large hospital compared to others in the area, such as Jefferson or the University of Penn.

My friend said when he first started selling hot dogs on that corner he sold about 250 to 300 a day. As the months went on Chris's business picked up considerably. Now he easily sells 600 to 700 hot dogs a day. And that doesn't include the chips, sodas, and assorted candy he offers as well.

How much does a pack of hot dogs cost? What if you went to a wholesale club and bought a few cases in bulk? You can find a case of twenty-four hot dogs for around $5; that's roughly 20¢ per hot dog. Let's play with some numbers here. We'll use ballpark figures to keep things simple.

If you sell each hot dog for $1, you make an 80¢ profit off each. Doesn't sound like much, does it? But let's go a little further: 100 hot dogs sold equals $80 profit; 300 hot dogs sold equals $240 profit. If you can sell at least 500 hotdogs a day (not the 600 to 700 we looked at earlier) you make a $400 profit.

Or maybe that's too many for you right away. But even if you sold, say 300 hot dogs a day, that's a $240 a day profit. Every ten days you earn $2,400; every twenty days $4,800; every thirty days (monthly) you'll see $7,200 in profits. That's $86,400 a year, not including profits on sales of chips, sodas, and candy. Excluding the operational cost associated with that of running a business.

How many people do you know personally who would like to make that type of money right now? If you think about it, you can. And it doesn't have to be hot dogs. Your food truck can sell whatever you think would turn a nice profit and sell well in the area.

Once your business is up and running, that's one thing you add to your asset column. What if you had two or three food stands? You should be thinking in terms of reinvesting the profits from the first asset into subsequent assets.

The joy of minding your own business and learning how it is run inside and out is that when you decide to hire employees to mind your business you already know what they should be doing day to day. You know the cost of inventory, and more importantly, you know the *net profit*—how much you have left after paying all expenses (cost of goods, employees, permits, fees, etc.).

I have a family member who opened a bakery. The concept was a great idea and the baked goods were delicious. However, the emotional attachment of wanting to make every item from scratch wasn't cost efficient. We suggested that they replace the daily cookies (make from scratch and very time consuming) with ready-made dough from a well-known brand. This brand was more cost efficient and just as good. They rejected this advice. These were the types of decisions along with an economic downturn that brought about the business' demise.

One of the core principles of The Money Game is to base your business decisions on the numbers. You can't allow the emotions of what you think is good to outweigh the numbers that tell you what is best, and most profitable. The most important factor is a positive outcome for your business model.

How about clothing? The same concept could be used for a retail clothing venture. You could look into the classified ads and find a reasonably priced storefront for lease. You could get your name incorporated and all the proper licenses exactly as we just discussed.

Now, remember earlier when we looked at the Magic Show convention? That could be a source of some inventory. Online, you could even develop your own designs in it and mix your style of fashion in with some of the more established names to gauge if you should start selling your own line of products. Women's clothing, accessories, and shoes always seem to have a huge potential for big profits.

The adult novelty industry is another source for big income that has a convention in Las Vegas. Women may do exceptionally well in this area since most women feel more comfortable around other women. You could sponsor adult toy parties. They could be in your home or you could rent a hotel suite two or three times a month and give your events.

One week you can sell clothes, one week do shoes and accessories, and the third week you can do the adult toys. It would be cost effective to give these events at home, but whatever is convenient for you.

I would strongly suggest that you take any and all profit and reinvest it into minding your own business. The more time and energy you put into minding your own business, the larger it will grow. Once you have established a clientele you are comfortable with, you are ready for the next step.

Your first step was playing The Money Game. You took that step in order to reach your goal—the big picture—of hiring employees to mind your business for you, ultimately making the transition from employee to employer. The reason you want to hire employees to run your company is so you have more free time for yourself to do whatever you like. You might even spend that time setting up more businesses in the beginning stages of your wealth building.

I strongly believe one of the best paths to becoming financially secure and obtaining wealth is to invest, reinvest, and then invest some more. By playing The Money Game you will be forcing your money to work harder and harder.

CHAPTER THIRTEEN

CREATE YOUR OWN ATM

I know there are a lot of people in college, or who have some type of college background, who are reading this book. In my opinion, that is a wonderful investment. It is an investment in yourself and your future. But the key is to reinvest, and unfortunately, most schools and colleges don't teach The Money Game.

For the most part, college is about teaching you the skills needed to find employment in the profession of your choice. However, these skills do not include showing you how to build a business out of your career choice. I am grateful for universities and know that they are important for the advancement of a productive society. Without college, there would be no doctors, lawyers, dentists, accountants, and a whole slew of other professions society needs in order to function.

After dropping out of school in the sixth grade, I am an advocate of academic education. I just think that financial education should be a prerequisite to choosing your college major. Building a business that can run and make a profit without your presence is a huge form of financial success. That means if you don't go to your place of business, it will still continue to operate without you.

Traditional academic learning focuses on one person doing all the work. If that person doesn't show up for work there is no business. Consider doctors, lawyers, and dentists. All three are great professions. But if the doctor doesn't go to the hospital, he doesn't get paid. If your attorney doesn't show up for court, he receives no legal fees. If the dentist doesn't fix your chipped tooth, guess what? He won't get paid. Learning the skills necessary for these types of career paths should be the foundation of building you own business.

For instance, if you are in medical school, would it be possible for you to become a pharmaceutical researcher and eventually come up with a drug to cure a certain illness and market that drug to the public? In doing this you would be providing a much-needed service to mankind and making good money from the royalties of the your pharmaceutical sales.

If you attend law school, your focus should be on making the transition from good lawyer to owner of a great law firm, a firm in which you have hired the best paralegals around and other attorneys fresh out of law school with top grades that you can employ to run your law firm.

If this is not your focus or way of thinking, then your path to wealth will undoubtedly be hard. However, if you can begin to think differently, make building your business the ultimate goal, and use your skills as the foundation, you are making the best use of your academic knowledge.

Learning The Money Game, your financial education will set you so far apart from the masses you won't believe it. First you must understand that not everybody wants to be an employer. Even a lot of top students, the ones who graduated with honors, will be satisfied with simply obtaining well-paying jobs.

There is nothing wrong with that—especially if those people are comfortable living that way. After all, it's what they learned to do in school. With your new way of thinking, your priority is to couple what you learned in school with your financial smarts and hire the best help to run the business.

Can you cook? I mean really well? Would you consider your-self one of the top ten chefs in your city? Why am I asking? Three words: culinary arts school. Think about this for a minute: What if you found a building or even an old restaurant? Then you find a chef who specializes in a very uncommon, yet delicious variety of dishes. You offer him a top chef position straight out of culinary arts school.

To sweeten the offer you could guarantee a bonus if the res-taurant meets a certain sales goal. In his contract, the chef under-stands that his salary is based solely on what the business gener-ates in income. Bingo! Found one. Now you have a restaurant with the basics already in place and a top chef with some unusual and delicious recipes that will add a new and exciting flavor (pun intended) to your new business.

This concept could be used for a barbershop and a hair salon as well. Can you find an old barbershop or hair salon in your area that you could bring back to life? Or even an old building you could lease with the option to buy? After putting in some chairs and touching the place up to suit your clientele base, you then go to barber and hair schools to scout new talent for your business.

Why not try a salon that caters to kids or even to seniors. In my experience, children and seniors would be much more comfort-able in an environment that specializes in providing them a good service.

The landscaping business also offers a very good opportunity to become an employer. There are lawns, bushes, trees, weeds, and grass everywhere. The good thing about this type of venture is that your start-up costs don't have to be too expensive. With some rakes, shovels, a few lawn mowers, and some hedge trimmers and invest in a few DVD's on the concepts of gardening and landscap-ing, you could be in business.

If you can get an inexpensive pickup truck from an auction or online, that would really help you get started. You would go through the same procedure to get your business license. Finding and hiring help wouldn't be hard since the requirements don't involve you having to look for individuals who graduated at the top of their class or even graduated at all. In the beginning, cutting grass, raking leaves, and shoveling snow would be all that's necessary to get your name out. You can also place ads on craigslist, you could have some of your satisfied customers to write reviews on Angie's list as well. You could canvas different communities and go door to door to find out who needs their grass cut or any type of lawn maintenance.

In the summer you could have contracts drawn up for your services to be rendered, say, once a week for $25 for small yards, and maybe $50 to $75 for larger yards. You would also figure out a schedule for the winter, all depending on the weather, of course.

Once you get enough customers in each community signed up for your business, you show your hired help how you want each yard done. You could work out a percentage from each yard contract to pay your help in the beginning stages. Say, $10 for small yards and $20 for large yards, to give your employees incentive to do as many yards as possible.

Let's look at some numbers. Say you find sixty customers and you have two employees. That's thirty yards for each employee. We'll say half the yards are small yards and the others are large. That comes to $750 for the small yards and $1,500 for the large ones, for a total of $2,250. After you deduct your employees' pay, you're left with $1,350 for that week's work—work that your employees did. That's $5,400 per month.

Keep in mind that was just one community. You could hire two more employees and do the same thing in another community. How about going to the churches or schools and getting large contracts to manicure their lawns? The possibilities go on and on.

Here's another idea: How about after building up your company's cash reserve you purchase a few used trucks or vans and incorporate a moving service with your landscaping business. What about purchasing something really big if you reinvest your profits back into your own business? All the while, creating a larger and larger asset.

I say that the truly rich do not work for money. That's because they understand inflation, taxes, and debt. The more money you make, the more money you lose in taxes and debt if you're not smart. Financial education teaches you how to convert phony money into real money as quickly as possible. This education also changes the way you look at money. In the Money Game, you see money from a more intelligent angle. This will help you transition your thinking from employee to employer.

As this takes place, your focus should shift to find ways to mind your own business that employs people rather than being an employee—providing housing instead of just consuming it. The best part is once you begin these things the government will reward you for being a producer. The government will also punish consumers who work for money by taxing them heavily. This will be explained in detail, in The Money Game 102.

CHAPTER FOURTEEN

MULTIPLE STREAMS
OF INCOME

By playing The Money Game, I finally found a way to make creating wealth and having the finer things in life a little easier. And most times after the initial setup, you don't have to do much work. Some people might call it a secret but it's no secret at all. It's called passive income.

There are basically two types of income: earned income and passive income. When you have a job, or work every day for a salary or particular profit, that is earned income. On the other hand, passive income is funds that come in from your investments and continue to come in whether you go to work or not.

Examples of passive income are multifamily properties that produce a profit, businesses that have a profitable return, and stocks that go up in value and produce dividends. I like passive income because it doesn't require you to have to keep doing something over and over in order to receive money. A lot of times when you focus on your job, career, or chosen profession, you lose sight of multiple streams of income because all of your time is used furthering your career. That's why passive income is so convenient.

The Internet offers an excellent opportunity for passive income. You could get a turnkey Internet business. Simply search "investment opportunities" and look further into the ones that capture your interest. That's a business model that is basically already set up for you. You select the product you want to sell, complete the ready-made website template or design your own, and congratulations! You are minding your own business and you have a potential passive income stream.

You can hire companies to manage your website, do web maintenance, or host your Internet business for a small monthly fee. You can even have your marketing and promotions handled by professionals in those fields. So there is no need to be a computer tech, electrode nerd, or have your masters in computer sciences to have your own online business.

Another source of passive income is a vending business. You can buy or lease your machines, stock them with items likely to appeal to your clientele, and place them in locations with high foot traffic, for example hospitals, college campuses, jails, hair salons, large waiting rooms, just about anywhere people pass by regularly.

You could also try leasing a video game. Trust me, a video game can do wonders at supplementing additional business income. I have a family member, Gigi that ran a beauty salon. She was able to cover most of the salon's utilities with the income that came from a simple multiscreen video game.

Let's say you have a couple thousand dollars. You could go to an auction and purchase a dump truck or a four-by-four used for hauling trash. I'm sure you could find a few guys who could use some work to drive or haul your trash around to different sites based on whatever contracts you have found.

In Philadelphia, a forty-foot Dumpster costs just north of $710. That can be rather expensive for small contractors on a strict budget. Many contractors would seriously consider subcontracting debris cleanup in order to save $100 or $200. By playing The

Money Game, you'll be overwhelmed with the demand for your services.

Once you have enough contracts, you can purchase another truck. Now you have a dump truck or waste management business.

Think of passive income streams like multiple faucets pouring money into one container (your pockets). When you have completed the initial setup (purchasing equipment and tools, finding workers, etc.) and your business starts running, the goal is for your employees to be able to mind your business without you physically being there.

There are services available to assist you with minding your business. You can hire a virtual assistant (VA) to handle any research online, set up appointments, schedule meetings, and basically anything else you can think of that doesn't require a physical presence. The cost of these assistants starts at $4 per hour for a VA based overseas, and $20 per hour for a VA based in the United States or Canada. The costs vary depending on the task you want done.

You could start your own research company and outsource (use somebody else's company) to do your research for cheaper than what you charge. Let's say I start a company called YouResearch. com and I charge $20 per hour to do a wide variety of research. I can hire a VA to do all the research I offer for, say, $4 to $5 per hour. Now all I do is focus on advertising and getting my clientele. I make as much as a $15 profit per hour while delegating all tasks to someone else.

I had a full-service salon in Philadelphia located in a section called Allegheny West. It was a good move during the late '80s and early '90s. The profit potential was huge. The industry has since become oversaturated. At this particular time, the concept was good, but the basic fundamentals of having someone else mind my business after I set it up were not my goal. Thus, I put much time and energy into physically being at the salon instead of delegating tasks and focusing more of my time on creating other income streams.

Through multiple trials, errors and mismanaging, I have learned numerous lessons from that experience, The greatest lesson was learning the difference between running a business versus working a job.

Once you become creative, your income potential is limitless. The key is not to focus on how much profit you can make as long as the business can run itself. Whatever the profit is, that's a plus if you are not going into your pocket or using any business reserves.

I ran this scenario past a friend of mine (let's call him Bret) last week, and his focus was on the amount of profit you make, as opposed to the amount of time you save. Understand this: your time is more valuable than the money you save by doing labor that can be done by someone else.

Here is Bret's viewpoint: He drives trucks for a living. When he graduated from trucking school and got his commercial driver's license, he started making roughly $500 per day, and he works every other day. He earns around $2,000 per week. This takes up his whole day on the days he works. And on his off days, he has to rest and prepare for the next day of work.

At this rate, Bret has no time to work on creating any other income streams because he doesn't have the energy or willpower since he is always drained from the day before. I suggested that he purchase a used truck and hire a driver to do his runs for him. I then explained two options.

Option 1: Purchase a truck for about $12,500 from an auction. (If you do some homework, you can find excellent deals at auctions, which will help you build your assets faster.) Find contracts for runs for his truck for $2,200 a week. Weekly maintenance on the truck would be about $250 to $350, and an average salary for a driver would be about $1,100 a week. So after paying expenses, the profit would be $800 to $900 a week.

Option 2: Lease a truck for $600 to $700 a week (maintenance included). Now, with the same driver's salary of $1,100 a week and the same $2,200 weekly contract, after paying expenses, the profit would be $500 to $600.

You can probably guess that Bret didn't like Option 2. Actually, he had a few choice words and mumbled some other pleasantries that wouldn't be suitable around anyone's kids, grandparents, or during a religious service.

It may sound crazy, but I actually like Option 2 because of the freedom it offers. Remember that Option 1 had a weekly maintenance fee of $250 to $350. And that's just regular upkeep. But what happens when something a little more serious happens to your truck? You not only use the little bit of cash you would be making next week, but you now have to devote your free time to getting your truck in order. And if it's something that requires a few days' work (and most major repairs would), you risk losing your contract. Now you have wasted time and money, and your whole operation becomes a possible failure.

With Option 2 you may only be making $500 to $600 profit weekly, but you know that if something happens with the truck, it's included in your maintenance fees, so your business still rolls on. And the extra time you save during the week can be used to find another contract, lease another truck, and hire another driver.

The more contracts, the more income. With some uncommon sense, Bret could lease three trucks, secure three contracts, and hire three drivers. If Bret played The Money Game he could make the same, if not more, money as he did driving himself *and* have more free time on his hands to do whatever he desired.

When we put our focus and energy on multiple streams of income, this is the end result. You can apply this example to a wide variety of business. All it takes is thinking differently. Work smarter, not harder, to accumulate assets, and those assets will buy more assets or pay for any of your liabilities. The Money Game can change your hard work to smart work.

CHAPTER FIFTEEN

IF IT WALKS LIKE A DUCK

Let's be real. Being broke sucks! Whoever said that money can't buy happiness probably never had any money themselves. I'm not saying that making money should be your sole purpose in life, because you can find happiness in many other things, but money certainly makes life more enjoyable. It also allows you to free up your time to exercise options that becomes available to indulge more leisurely pleasures.

If you are broke, need money, can't catch a break, are doing bad, or whatever you want to call it, let me be blunt with you: you need to change your friends. In order to find success you better *change* your friends, or change your *friends*. In other words, either change the way the people around you think or change the people you surround yourself with every day.

There is a lot of truth in the old cliché "birds of a feather flock together." Employees usually hang out with employees, lawyers run with other lawyers, criminals with criminals, doctors with doctors, and so forth. The thing is, once you pay attention to this pattern you'll also notice that entrepreneurs associate with entrepreneurs, and successful people from all walks travel some of the same circles. Once you learn the Money Game your circle will change.

You have to get in where you fit in. So the question is, where do you fit in? If things are not the way you want them to be right now you better start fitting in someplace else. Different circles attract different people—usually people with the same mindset and attitude about life.

Different circles also speak a different language. For example, an employee might say, "I work so hard I deserve a raise" or "I wish we had longer breaks." A person who minds his own business might say, "It's hard to find good help."

There are many ways to meet likeminded people. You could attend functions or events sponsored by people who have similar interests. Become a member of a successful club, or learn a new vocabulary. Learn the business or lingo of the people you want in your circle or whose circle you want to be a part of and soon enough you will meet new friends.

List six people besides coworkers and family whom you spend the most time with. Now determine which circle they are in. Since your friends are mirrors into your own character, this should give you a clear reflection of yourself. Do you like what you see? If you do, then congratulations! But if you don't, then you need to make some changes.

I recall a few years back when I was invited to attend a monthly meeting of an investment group by a family member, Lee Lee. The meetings were held at Lee Lee's coworker's (Mark's) house. The group was made up of individuals of various backgrounds. All shared the common goal of exploring the possibilities by getting their feet wet at making some sound investments. I believe that I learned a great deal by attending those group meeting. I highly recommend such investment group. Each individual brings something unique that can possibly provide a benefit.

Now listen, by no means am I saying you should dump your old friends. What I am saying is if you are really serious about achieving your financial dreams, then you should meet new people and expand your world. Change your old ways of thinking, sharpen your financial education, and play The Money Game.

Sometimes we just have to do something different in order to reach our goals. I had a buddy, let's call him Rich, who always seemed to have a new source to get his inventory from. Even when times were bad, Rich still was able to provide his business associates with consignment. He was able to do this because

(1) He was constantly expanding his circle (networking); and
(2) He used a different approach than his peers when it came to finding inventory.

Most people in Rich's line of work waited around for handouts and just had to accept whatever inventory and prices were given to them. On the other hand, Rich understood The Money Game and was what one calls a go-getter. He wasn't afraid to travel and take chances.

I remember times when Rich would take long trips to go to auctions, seminars, and other venues that he thought were suitable for mixing and mingling with a different circle. He would network and create new sources of inventory for his business simply by expanding his contacts.

This way of thinking can be applied to all walks of life and many different professions. Once we are able to get past the initial fear of playing The Money Game we can begin to focus on exactly how money works and start creating new ways to have income flowing in.

Do you know anybody who just took everything they had and moved to another city? You have to really believe in yourself to do something like that. My experience has shown me that those particular individuals are usually the most successful in life. You know why? They're willing to put themselves in a "do or die" situation. They create a situation for themselves in which failure is not an option. When placed in these situations you would be amazed at how creative the mind gets. There is no comfort at sailing out into the ocean alone where you can no longer see the shore.

I remember reading about Yiptun, a commander in the Spartan army. Yiptun was known for his fearlessness and his ability to win seemingly impossible battles. The one battle that stood out to me the most was when Yiptun, who had an army of about ten thousand soldiers, faced a rival army that was also ten thousand strong. Yiptun took his army on a very long journey across several seas to a foreign land to fight his rival.

The problem was the journey was so long, and since he had never actually been to this foreign land, during the trip his soldiers ran out of food and became weak and feeble. Many even died. When Yiptun finally reached the bank of his adversary's land, he ordered his entire army out of the boats that had carried them across the seas. Then Yiptun set the ships on fire.

As the ships burned, Yiptun turned to what was left of his tired and famished army—with no way to retreat and no way to sail back to their homeland—and simply said, "We will win this battle and take over this land. Or we will die." Given those choices, failure was not an option.

You have to approach businesses, investments, partnerships, work, and everything else that is important to you with this same passion. Women seem to be able to make this transition a little easier than men. I had two female friends (Sun and Pump) who were out of work and couldn't find new employment in Philadelphia. They hopped on a plane and moved to Cali. No job lined up, no family, not much cash, nothing.

As a matter of fact, the one I sometimes keep in touch with found employment as a stylist not long after the day she arrived. Sun made a decent living acting and modeling. What I do know is that they never returned to live in Philadelphia. The point is, there comes a time when you have to wake up and realize that you must take your life in a different direction. The only question is, are you willing to do it?

THE OTHER SIDE OF TRAGEDY

A woman by the name of Mimi. Mimi focused on being the perfect wife, completely submissive to her husband, whom she loved with all her heart. Stan, her husband, focused on providing for his family and maintaining a well-paid job. The fall of the economy and the rising unemployment rate took an unfortunate toll on their family. Stan lost his job. Unable to effectively cope with these lifestyle changes, Stan began drinking himself into a stupor every night, as well as beating Mimi as a pastime.

One night, arriving home in his usual drunken state, Stan became angry with Mimi because she did not have his dinner prepared on time. This was a fairly regular occurrence. Whenever Stan got drunk, he found some reason to be angry and displeased with Mimi, which usually ended with a beating with Mimi on the receiving end.

On this particular night, Mimi decided to stand up to him. Something inside her realized she could take no more. She hit Stan in the face with an iron and ran into the bathroom and locked the door. Mimi, fearing his wrath, called the police. Stan vowed to kill her before he would go to prison. Breaking down the door, Stan stabbed Mimi numerous times. Mimi woke up days later in a hospital room with tubes and monitors attached to her body. As for Stan, he had been arrested for assault.

A social worker visited with Mimi and obtained information concerning her relatives, anticipating her release to them. Mimi explained she was originally from Philadelphia and had moved to Florida several years before. She had no immediate family or close relatives, except for her in-laws, with whom she was not on speaking terms.

Mimi had two options: she could either return to Philadelphia or live in a protected women's shelter locally. Mimi chose the latter. She went to the shelter in a depressed state, damaged by the difficulties and the anticipation of an uncertain future.

Mimi's stay in the women's shelter proved to be beneficial both physically and mentally. The women at the shelter encouraged her to participate in a physical therapy program, which enabled her to regain her physical strength and baseline abilities. She also attended the weekly group therapy sessions and was able to share her story as well as listen to the stories of the other women.

During the group meetings, each of the women shared her own tragic story of being brutally abused by a partner. One day, the group counselor gave Mimi her car keys to retrieve some donuts from the counselor's car. Mimi noticed that the key chain had a canister of Mace on it. Mimi was intrigued, asking the counselor where she might be able to obtain a similar canister. The counselor informed Mimi she had bought the canister during a recent trip to New York.

This motivated Mimi to start a business she called Little Helpers, selling small security gadgets, each on a key chain. Her product line included Mace and pepper spray, stun guns, loud horns, and similar devices that women could find invaluable. MiMi invested the $600 she saved during her stay at the women's shelter in her pursuit of her new business venture. She grew her business, finding a distributor on the Internet that was located in Chinatown, New York City. Mace and pepper spray cost her $3 per unit, which she retailed for $7. The stun guns cost $11, selling for $25. Horns cost $5, selling for $10.

Things started off slowly for the first few weeks before gaining momentum, eclipsing even Mimi's best hopes or expectations. She found it necessary to hire a few employees. Mimi closed out her first year in business with a net profit of $125,000! Furthermore, once she realized that she could make this a true business venture instead of a side hustle to make a few extra dollars, Mimi went to a local lawyer and sought her advice on which business entity would be most suitable for her venture. She was advised to start a S sub chapter corporation, which turned out to be sound advice.

Like in the above story, Mimi was able to peep game in her need to change her circumstances. Your story doesn't have to begin in tragedy in order for you to spot a move, take action, and capitalize on it. In The Money Game, although the ideas may change the concepts and principles remain the same. How many times have you come up with different ideas and procrastinated to a point that they were placed far back in your mind? If you make a sound decision in your life and play The Money Game, those same ideas can be given a life that expands the context of your financial well-being. At some point you can find a niche that works. Get in the game!

CHAPTER SIXTEEN

INSTANT GRATIFICATION

Does the phrase "Keeping up with the Joneses" sound familiar to you? That's probably because you have tried to do so in the past, or are attempting to do so right now. Today, the phrase just has different names: "stuntin'," "flossin'," "ballin'," "makin' it rain," or whatever you want to call it. That has to be the most foolish thing we can ever do with our money.

I know I was one of the biggest fools out there. When a new Benz came out, I got it. New Lorinser rims? Got 'em. I remember back in the '90s when the then famous club in Philly Studio 37 first opened. I had to be there right after I hit King of Prussia Mall and grabbed something new to wear. All the latest kicks, new jewelry every four or five months, not to mention a new vehicle to go with it. And all for what? A big show!

It's sad, but we spend most of our time (and money) trying to impress people who don't really care anything about us. I'm not saying that you shouldn't or can't have these nice things, but you shouldn't go broke trying to acquire these things either. We should get these creature comforts after we have set up income streams to pay for the luxuries we want.

That's right, ladies, as soon as those new Louboutin red-bottom shoes hit the store, you should *not* run out and get them! And gentlemen, put a hold on every flavor of the new Guseppe shoes. Purchase something that will bring some money in with the same cash you would have used for those luxuries, and once you have made a profit from your purchase, use that profit to buy what you want to splurge on.

For the most part, our thought process has been tainted. The saying is very true that everything that glitters ain't gold. Just because you see a guy driving a Benz doesn't mean he's got money. The nice pair of Chanel shoes that she had on could have been knock-offs. All that cash you see guys tossing in the bar or strip club could be their entire paycheck. All smoke and mirrors.

I had a buddy named Prada RIP who stayed fresh. I mean all the time. He drove a 600 Mercedes-Benz, lived in a luxurious home in the suburbs, and wore expensive jewelry. But more often than not, he didn't know how he was going to make the payments on most of the trinkets of his lavish lifestyle. He had the masses fooled, and to him, it seemed to be worth the headache he got each month around bill time.

On the opposite end of the spectrum, I had another friend, a little more low-key than Prada, so let's call him Pac. My friend Pac absolutely refused to drive around in luxury vehicles. And it's not like he didn't have the financial means, because he actually owned a car lot. I remember when a few of the guys from our neighborhood who were enjoying large amounts of street profits would get together and poke fun at how Pac had all this money and only spent it on more ordinary cars for his car lot.

Well, years went by and gradually those Maxima's, Altima's, and Corollas in my friend's car lot became Lexus's, BMWs, and Mercedes. Not only was he buying more and more vehicles to sell (assets), he was also purchasing homes that needed rehabbing for very cheap. He bought homes for $10,000 to $20,000 back when houses were readily available to everyone. Then, after doing mostly cosmetic renovations, those same houses were worth $90,000 to $120,000.

I'll never forget a particular conversation I had with Pac where he was upset that some guy only wanted to give him $750,000 cash for some property that he owned free and clear. This conversation stood out to me because at that time you were considered rich or "doing your thing" if you had $250,000. Maybe even $100,000. And Pac had the audacity to be upset with a "measly" three quarters of a million dollar offer. I think it was around that time that I started to change my outlook on money.

The more discipline we have, or are able to exercise, the better we can control our desires for instant gratification. We should never *not* get the things we want in life. But it's *how* we get them that makes all the difference. The people that think they will save for years and then invest in some great opportunity are in for a rude awakening.

When you really think about it, isn't it crazy for people to believe they will always have their entire lives ahead of them? We all know that death often comes out of nowhere. And none of us knows when it will come for us. Yet, people still believe the illusion that they have lots of time ahead of them. So they constantly put off investing. "I'll look into it." "I've got time." "I'll check it out tomorrow." These are all popular excuses to not become wealthy. Some people use these over and over until one day-old age creeps up and they look back and realize they haven't done anything to achieve financial freedom.

What would you do if your days were numbered? Well, here's a little secret. In all actuality, they are! But most of us only come to this realization when there is very little time left, and then, my friend, it is too late.

So you must be willing to focus on what you can do *now* so that you will be able to reap your rewards sooner *and* later. That focus should undoubtedly be on assets. This mental concentration and focus is a key to success in so many facets of living. The stronger your focus, the more effective you'll be able to work. Your thought process will be totally different. You'll see things that others don't.

Have you ever heard the saying, "There's nothing new under the sun?" It's true. The thing is, most rich or successful people have learned to pay attention to details. They are able to spot a move or trend and jump on it. Do you remember the concept of the peeping game? This is where it applies; they see a void and fill it. They know how to think in terms of making money multiply, not spending it on liabilities or watching their savings dwindle away.

CHAPTER SEVENTEEN

REAL ESTATE

My personal favorite way to become wealthy is through real estate. Especially if you've been turned off by the country's financial downturn and want to invest in a more concrete asset. No matter what the economy is doing, no matter how bad people's finances get, or how much the unemployment rate rises, everybody has to live somewhere.

I have loved real estate since back when I first started playing the Money Game. The object is to buy as many properties as possible, fix them up to be able to get as much rent as you can, then lease your property and collect your rent. The more property you have, the more money you collect.

If you think you have to be a real estate agent to make a lot of money in real estate, you don't. Real estate investors are the ones who make a lot of money in this field.

You may have heard of an old fella who goes by the name Donald Trump. He is a multibillionaire. And he gained his fortune primarily through real estate. He has more money than probably any real estate agent you know, or have ever heard of, and he doesn't even have a real estate license. He's an investor who hires real estate agents to find properties for him to buy.

There are many strategies people use to make money in real estate, but for the purpose of this book, we will focus on the buy-and-hold concept.

Flipping houses—buying properties that need some work, fixing them up, and selling them for a quick profit—became very popular in Philadelphia in the late '90s. So much so that many states decided that people were abusing this trend by evading certain tax penalties. Now there are laws preventing you from flipping more than a certain amount of properties per year. But I think that was a blessing in disguise.

Most of the time, when people do flip a property, they don't reinvest the profit. They are so happy with the amount they made over what they originally paid for the property, they go out and splurge on cars, clothes, and jewelry. The problem was (and still is) what happens when all that splurging comes to an end? Now you have no property, no income, and all too often, you don't even have enough money to purchase another property to flip. You must preserve your working capital to play The Money Game.

That's why I'm a big fan of buying property and keeping it. Once you buy or get control of your first property, you can use that as a foundation for building your empire. The reason I like to buy and hold versus selling my property is because you can use the property as your own personal bank.

Let me give you an example: Say you buy a house at auction for $10,000. You do some cosmetic work and basic renovating that costs you an additional $15,000. You have an appraiser come out and the house is now valued at $70,000.

Now, you can choose Option 1 and sell the house for $60,000 to $65,000 to get a sale fast and take your one-time profit of $35,000 to $45,000. Or you can choose Option 2 and refinance the house (take a loan out on the property) and maybe get an 80 to 90 percent loan to value (LTV). That's how much the bank will loan you depending on what the property is worth. (Note: With the current economic downturn, the LTV may have been lowered to 70 to 75 percent. The Money Game concept remains the same.)

Let's continue with our house valued at $70,000. If you get 80 percent of the value, the bank would loan you $56,000 (80 percent x $70,000); or if you could get 90 percent of the value, the bank would loan you $63,000 (90 percent x $70,000). You would then have a mortgage on the house of roughly $500 to $600 a month. With Option 1 you take your profit once and that's it. With Option 2, by keeping the property and refinancing, you get the $56,000 or $63,000 and if you put a tenant inside the property to pay back the loan it's all yours tax-free!

And here's the icing on the cake: once the loan is repaid, you can do the same thing over and over. I would strongly suggest that you reinvest in more property. I like multifamily properties because of the income they can produce. Always remember, a steady stream of income plays a substantial part to your becoming wealthy.

There are many traditional and non-traditional ways to find suitable investment properties. From attending a public auction or as simple as getting a lead from a neighbor. At times, I would put the word out amongst my neighbors that I'd give up to $500as a finder's fee for any property they led me to that resulted in a purchase. Once you begin your journey at playing The Money Game, real estate investment opportunities will begin to surface frequently. I found myself turning down many good opportunities because there were so many. *The Money Game 102* will go more in depth about finding good real estate investment opportunities.

Multiunit properties allow you to pay back a loan you have on a property with one, maybe two of the units, and the other one or two units could be a source of income. If you have a few properties like this you can easily have a steady stream of cash that will never end.

AFTERWORD

It has been my intention to make this book as interesting as possible and at the same time give you some serious insight on money and how to play The Money Game. I wrote this book hoping to share some of the game and money lessons I learned the hard way. I went through numerous trials and errors so you don't have to.

Always remember that at a certain height there are no clouds. If there *are* clouds in your life, it is because your mind hasn't soared high enough. Change your old ways of thinking and *get in the game.*

We have kept the concepts simple in *The Money Game 101.* As you go through the series, you will become a Money Game player. We have kept these books short and to the point because many people are not convinced they have the time to invest in their financial security. We must transcend beyond what seems like insurmountable obstacles into the exploration of financial literacy.

Let's change our minds!

INTRO TO MONEY GAME 102

The Money Game series is based on a conscious effort to introduce an uncomfortable subject: financial literacy. It's a sensitive yet complex issue that the common man had been left to deal with his or her everyday life. No longer are the days of mediocrity of just getting by good enough. The time has come for us to step up and claim responsibility for our economic situation. To ensure our well-being and financial security our actions must be based on well-informed decision making. Financial security has become a distant thought because many of us are pessimistic about going the traditional route to accumulating wealth. *The Money Game 102 is* about attainable way to make ensured investments. Ensured in the sense that you increase your chances of success and decrease your chances of falling. Of course nothing is guaranteed, but with the due diligence that you will learn in *The Money Game 102*, you can bypass many of the mistakes that the novice investor makes.

In today's market dollars are tight. There is much less room for the mistakes of the past. Money Game players need and deserve great value for their hard-earned buck. We can't sit on the sideline and allow our money to stagnate while losing value. We must take a position of action and become investors in pursuit of our financial well-being. the term investor, I'm speaking about individuals who acquire assets and mind their own business. Sometimes I sit back and reminisce about my long journey to financial literacy.

Ironically I became an investor (at least that's what I believed at the same time) in my teenage years. I was introduced to the world of investing by an unscrupulous or what some would call shady character. At one time I considered this individual to be a mentor. My mentor (let's call him Twan) was more focused on getting over and lining his own pockets with light hard-earned pennies than teaching me the core principles of the Money Game. I recall one incident in particular when I purchased my first single-family home. I purchased the property from no other than Twan! I was very excited to be purchasing my first of many homes to come. Led by emotions, I allowed Twan to take advantage of what I didn't know and understand at that time. One of the first issues of many that followed was that the property was next to a vacant house. This made the property extremely difficult to be insured. This is something Twan was aware of, but failed to share with me. To make a long story short, I was under the impression that I bought the property for less than $20,000 (completely renovated). As it turns out it was a money pit and I spent at least an additional $100,000 in that property before I conceded to defeat and decided to get rid of it by selling it.

Like me at the time, financially uninformed investors base most of their decisions on emotions. The financially informed have an entrance and exit strategy before they make a purchase. Throwing good money after bad is one of the most common mistakes for the novice investor. As my life as an ill-informed investor continued on I did get better at making decisions, however my emotions continued to play a big part in those decisions. In the world of investing to create assets, on-the-job training is like running up a hill. I'm not saying it can't be done but one of the core principles of The Money Game is to work smarter not harder. I can't stress the importance of making an investment in your financial education. It increases your odds of winning tenfold. The Twans of the world would hate for you to learn anything that levels the playing field. It took me several years to come to the realization that Twan didn't have my best interest at heart.

One of the biggest mistakes that a Money Game player can make is to base his or her investment decisions on emotions. It doesn't matter if that emotion is love, fear, or greed. That's what The Money Game 102 is about. We must use our God-given intellect in order to increase our financial literacy. I'm sure that most of you have tested the waters of investing even if it was as simple as opening a lemonade stand. Hopefully when you tested those waters you didn't run into somebody like Twan. Unfortunately the world is full of Twans today.

Only through financial literacy can we protect ourselves from becoming the next victim of such unscrupulous individuals. I learned the hard way and I hope through my experiences you won't have to as well. Somehow I got lucky and managed to pull through (just barely) while throwing good money after bad. Often my emotions would lead me into circumstances that made what started out as an investment no different than going to Vegas and betting it all at a craps table. My young life as an investor went on like that for many years. I found myself trusting people on a whim and prayer. I was illiterate both academically and financially. There was no way I was capable of understanding the difference at the time. However, I always possessed a drive and desire within me to win. I had the will to do what's necessary. Yet my good spirits and drive continued to hit many bumps on the road.

Can you begin to imagine what life was like before man invented the wheel? Being exploited because of a lack of knowledge is one of the worst feelings imaginable. I'm glad there came a time when I met someone, let's call her Angel. She helped me take steps to change that. I went back to school and got my GED. I was proud of my accomplishment but I also understood that it was just the beginning of my journey.

I began to read various books on the subjects and I came to notice a pattern. The Twans of the world were out in full force. Headlines like "TLC Files for Bankruptcy After Selling 10 Million Plus Albums!" and "So and So Hit the Lottery for Millions and Now They Are Broke Three Years Later!" We all know people who play the lottery religiously waiting on that big payday. The big question for me was how these people could attain all this success and riches only to end up broke and back to rubbing nickels together. We can't confuse common thinking with common sense. When I sit back and reflect on all the miscalculations and common mistakes that I made on account of what I didn't know or understand all I can do is laugh at myself. I did that to keep from crying by the way.

The Money Game 101 is a set of simple rules for people who want to get their feet wet in investing or those seeking out the first level of financial security. The Money Game 102 is a transitional set of concepts that take you to the next level of increasing wealth and financial understanding. While the core principles and concepts can be easily understood, make no mistake about the fact that you will be increasing your financial IQ the more you read. All of the investments that you will learn are ones a semi novice can comfortably make if you possess the desire to change your financial situation. I invite all the Money Game players on a journey to the next level: *The Money Game 102…*

Sample Letter # 1

Date:

Credit Bureau (Insert Name Here)
Address (company address)
RE: (Account Number)

Dear (Credit Bureau Name),

I have just received my credit report and have noted that it contains erroneous information regarding the following accounts. I would like them deleted from my record.

Collection Account_____. This is not correct, please remove.

ABC Mortgage- This is not mine.

123 Gas Company (acct #_____) When I questioned 123 Gas Company about this account, they told me they requested this to be removed from my credit report. How were you able to confirm it?

MasterCard (acct #_____) this is not mine.

Please reinvestigate and delete these disputed items. 30 days constitutes a reasonable time to check these out. Please notify me if it takes longer. Please send names and business addresses of those persons you contacted for any verification. Also, as per the Fair Credit Reporting Act, please send me notification that the items have been deleted. Please send an updated copy of my credit report to the following address:

Sincerely,

Name
Address
Social Security Number

Sample Letter #2

Date: _____
Collection Agent:_____
Address: _____

Re: Account :_____

To whom it may concern;

When living in Pennsylvania, I received service through XYZ Telephone Company. During that time, there were numerous billing errors. My records were repeatedly mixed up with another account holder. Though time consuming and aggravating, the phone company always found and corrected the errors.

Before moving to New Jersey, I stopped service and paid the final bill. I never thought I would continue to be plagued with XYZ Telephone company errors.

I am sure if you speak with a live representative at XYZ Telephone Company, there will be a record of the problems we experienced with the billing. I am also certain you will discover that this is not my debt.

Though I was assured by the telephone company at the time that my name was not the cause of the errors, I am not so sure.

I would truly appreciate your assistance.

Sincerely,

Your Name
Address

Sample Letter #3

Date: _____

Company Name:_____

Address:_____

Re: Unauthorized Credit Report Inquiry

Dear 555 Credit Card Company,

I have received a copy of my credit report from (credit bureau name). The credit report showed a credit inquiry by your company that I do not recall authorizing. I understand, under my rights, you do not have permission to add an inquiry on to my credit file unless I give my permission. I request that this inquiry be removed from my credit file.

I am also requesting that you forward me documentation stating that this unauthorized inquiry has been removed from my credit report.

If you find that I am incorrect on the above stated matter, then please send me proof to the address listed above.

Thank You,

Your signature

Your name

BIOGRAPHIES

Tim Allen

Born in Denver, Colorado, Allen is the son of Martha Katherine (née Fox), a community-service worker, and Gerald M. Dick, a real estate agent. He is the third oldest of five brothers. His father died in a car accident, colliding with a drunk driver, when Allen was eleven. Two years later, his mother married her high school sweetheart, a successful business executive, and moved with her six children to Birmingham, Michigan, a suburb of Detroit, to be with her new husband and his three children. Allen attended Ernest W. Seaholm High School in Birmingham, where he was in theater and music classes (resulting in his love of classical piano). He then attended Central Michigan University and transferred to Western Michigan University in 1974. At Western Michigan, Allen worked at the student radio station WIDR and received a Bachelor of Science degree in communications specializing in radio and television production in 1976 with a split minor in philosophy and design. In 1998, Western Michigan awarded Allen an honorary fine arts degree and the Distinguished Alumni Award.

On October 2, 1978, Allen was arrested in the Kalamazoo/ Battle Creek International Airport for possession of over 650 grams (1.4 pounds) of cocaine. He subsequently pleaded guilty to drug trafficking charges, and provided the names of other dealers in exchange for a sentence of three to seven years rather than a possible life imprisonment. He was paroled on June 12, 1981, after serving two years and four months in a federal correctional institution, Sandstone, in Sandstone, Minnesota. Allen had the Federal Bureau of Prisons Register #04276-040.

Allen was raised as an Episcopalian. He was married to Laura Diebel from April 7, 1984, until they legally separated in 1999. Their divorce was finalized in 2003.They have a daughter, Katherine, born in 1989. Allen married actress Jane Hajduk on October 7, 2006, in a small private ceremony in Grand Lake, Colorado. They had dated for five years.

Tyler Perry

Tyler Perry (born September 14, 1969) is an American actor, director, screen and playwright, producer, author, and songwriter. Perry wrote and produced many stage plays during the 1990s and early 2000s. In 2005, he released his first film, *Diary of a Mad Black Woman.* In 2011, *Forbes* named him the highest paid man in entertainment, earning $130 million between May 2010 and 2011.

Perry was born in New Orleans, Louisiana, as Emmitt Perry, Jr. His family consisted of three siblings, his mother, Willie Maxine Perry (née Campbell), and his father, Emmitt Perry, Sr., a carpenter. Perry once said his father's "only answer to everything was to beat it out of you." As a child, Perry once went so far as to attempt suicide in an effort to escape his father's beatings. In contrast to his father, his mother took him to church each week, where he sensed a certain refuge and contentment. At age sixteen, he had his first name legally changed from Emmitt to Tyler in an effort to distance himself from his father.

Many years later, after seeing the film *Precious*, he was moved to relate for the first time accounts of being molested by a friend's mother at age ten; he was also molested by three men previous to this, and later found out his own father had molested his friend.

While Perry did not complete high school, he earned a GED. In his early twenties, watching an Oprah Winfrey talk show, he heard someone describe the sometimes therapeutic effect that the act of writing can have, enabling the author to work out his or her own problems. This comment inspired him to apply himself to a career in writing. He soon started writing a series of letters to himself, which became the basis for the musical *I Know I've Been Changed*.

J. K. Rowling

Joanne "Jo" Rowling, (born July 31, 1965), better known as J. K. Rowling, is a British novelist, famous for writing the *Harry Potter* fantasy series. The books have gained worldwide attention, won multiple awards, sold more than four hundred million copies to become the best-selling book series in history, and have been the basis for a popular series of films, in which Rowling had overall approval on the scripts as well as maintaining creative control by serving as a producer on the final installment. Rowling conceived the idea for the series on a train trip from Manchester to London in 1990.

Rowling has led a "rags to riches" life story, in which she progressed from living on social security to multimillionaire status within five years. As of March 2011, when its latest world billionaires list was published, *Forbes* estimated Rowling's net worth to be US$1 billion. The 2008 *Sunday Times* Rich List estimated Rowling's fortune at £560 million ($798 million), ranking her as the twelfth richest woman in the United Kingdom. *Forbes* ranked Rowling as the forty-eighth most powerful celebrity of 2007, and *Time* magazine named her as a runner-up for its 2007 Person of the Year, noting the social, moral, and political inspiration she has given her fans. In October 2010, J. K. Rowling was named Most Influential Woman in Britain by leading magazine editors. She has become a notable philanthropist, supporting such charities as Comic Relief, One Parent Families, Multiple Sclerosis Society of Great Britain, and Lumos (formerly the Children's High Level Group).

On April 12, 2012, Rowling announced that her new adult novel, *The Casual Vacancy*, would be published in the UK by Little, Brown & Company on September 27, 2012.

Although she writes under the pen name J. K. Rowling, pronounced like rolling, her name when her first *Harry Potter* book was published was simply Joanne Rowling. Fearing that the target audience of young boys might not want to read a book written by a woman, her publishers demanded that she use two initials, rather than her full name. As she had no middle name, she chose K as the second initial of her pen name, from her paternal grandmother Kathleen Ada Bulgen Rowling. She calls herself Jo and has said, "No one ever called me Joanne when I was young, unless they were angry." Following her marriage, she has sometimes used the name Joanne Murray when conducting personal business. During the Leveson Inquiry she gave evidence under the name of Joanne Kathleen Rowling.

Charles Dutton

Charles Stanley Dutton (born January 30, 1951) is an American stage, film, and television actor and director. He is perhaps best known for his roles as "Fortune" in the film *Rudy* and "Dillon" in *Alien 3*. He also starred in the television series *Roc* (1991–1994) and *House MD* (as the father of Eric Foreman).

Dutton was born on the east side of Baltimore, Maryland, In his youth, Dutton dropped out of school before finishing middle school. He had a short-lived stint as an amateur boxer with the nickname Roc. It was in prison, however, that he finally found his passion. When he was seventeen, he got into a fight that resulted in the death of a man Dutton claimed had attacked him. Dutton was charged and convicted of manslaughter, and he spent the next two years in prison. Several months after being released from prison, Dutton was arrested for possession of a deadly weapon and was sentenced to three years in prison.

Several months into his second prison term, Dutton was sentenced to six days of solitary confinement, which allowed prisoners to take one book. By accident, he grabbed an anthology of black playwrights. He enjoyed the plays so much that, upon his release from confinement, he petitioned the warden to start a drama group for the Christmas talent show. The warden agreed on the condition that Dutton go back to school and get his GED. Dutton accomplished that and went on to eventually complete a two-year college program at Hagerstown Junior College (now Hagerstown Community College) in Hagerstown, Maryland. Upon his release, he enrolled as a drama major at Towson State University (now known as Towson University) in the Baltimore suburb of Towson, Maryland.

After his time at Towson, Dutton earned a master's degree in acting from the Yale School of Drama.

Robert Johnson

Robert L. Johnson (born April 8, 1946) is an American business magnate best known for being the founder of television network Black Entertainment Television (BET), and he is also its former chairman and chief executive officer. Johnson is currently chairman and founder of RLJ Development and former majority owner of the Charlotte Bobcats, a National Basketball Association franchise, along with rapper Nelly and NBA legend and current majority owner Michael Jordan. In 2001, Johnson became the first African American billionaire and the first black person to be listed on any of *Forbes'* world's richest lists (excluding Canadian billionaire Michael Lee-Chin, who first appeared on the list the same year, who is of mixed black and Chinese ancestry).

Johnson was born in Hickory, Mississippi, but spent almost all of his childhood in Freeport, Illinois. He was the ninth of ten children born to Edna Johnson and Archie Johnson. Johnson graduated from Freeport High School in 1964. He studied history at the University of Illinois and graduated in 1968 with a bachelor's degree. While at the University of Illinois, Johnson was a member of the Beta chapter of Kappa Alpha Psi fraternity. He earned a master's degree in international affairs from the Woodrow Wilson School of Public and International Affairs at Princeton University.

From 1969 to 2002, he was married to Sheila Johnson. Together they founded the entertainment network BET, which they sold to Viacom in 2001.

In 1979, he left NCTA to create Black Entertainment Television, the first cable television network aimed at African Americans. It was launched in January 1980, initially broadcasting for two hours a week.

In 1991, BET became the first black-controlled company listed on the New York Stock Exchange. As of 2007, BET reaches more than 65 million US homes (according to biography.com) and expanded into other BET-related television channels that make up the BET Networks: BETJ, and digital cable channels BET Hip-Hop and BET Gospel.

In 2002, Johnson took the company private, buying back all of its publicly traded stock. In 2003, BET was no longer a black-owned business when Viacom bought it for $3 billion. Johnson's 63 percent stake made him worth over a billion dollars after taxes, making him the richest black person in the United States until he surrendered the title to Oprah Winfrey when his then-wife Sheila Johnson claimed much of his billion in divorce. Johnson continued to be the company's chairman and CEO for six years. In 2005, Johnson turned over the titles of president and chief operating officer of BET to Debra L. Lee, a former BET vice president.

Bill Gates

Microsoft's BASIC was popular with computer hobbyists, but Gates discovered that a premarket copy had leaked into the community and was being widely copied and distributed. In February 1976, Gates wrote an Open Letter to Hobbyists in the MITS newsletter saying that MITS could not continue to produce, distribute, and maintain high-quality software without payment. This letter was unpopular with many computer hobbyists, but Gates persisted in his belief that software developers should be able to demand payment. Microsoft became independent of MITS in late 1976, and it continued to develop programming language software for various systems. The company moved from Albuquerque to its new home in Bellevue, Washington on January 1, 1979, after the former rejected his loan application.

The idea that would spawn Microsoft germinated when Paul Allen showed Bill Gates the January 1, 1975 issue of *Popular Electronics* that demonstrated the Altair 8800. Allen and Gates saw potential to develop an implementation of the programming language BASIC for the system. Bill Gates called the creators of the new microcomputer, MITS (Micro Instrumentation and Telemetry Systems), offering to demonstrate the implementation in order to win a contract with the company. Allen and Gates had neither an interpreter nor an Altair system, yet in the eight weeks before the demo they developed an interpreter. When Allen flew to Albuquerque, New Mexico, to meet with MITS, the interpreter worked and MITS agreed to distribute Altair BASIC. Allen and Gates left Boston, moved to Albuquerque (where MITS was located), and cofounded Microsoft there. Gross income of the young company was $1 million in 1975.

During Microsoft's early years, all employees had broad responsibility for the company's business. Gates oversaw the business details, but continued to write code as well. In the first five years, Gates personally reviewed every line of code the company shipped, and often rewrote parts of it as he saw fit.

Mark Zuckerberg

Mark Elliot Zuckerberg (born May 14, 1984) is an American computer programmer and Internet entrepreneur. He is best known as one of four cofounders of the social networking site Facebook, of which he is chairman and chief executive. It was cofounded as a private company in 2004 by Zuckerberg and classmates Dustin Moskovitz, Eduardo Saverin, and Chris Hughes while they were students at Harvard University. Zuckerberg is the largest individual shareholder with 28.4 percent of the common stock and controls 56.9 percent of the voting power. As of 2012, his personal wealth was estimated at more than $19.1 billion, making him one of the world's youngest billionaires.

Zuckerberg launched Facebook from his Harvard dormitory room on February 4, 2004. An earlier inspiration for Facebook may have come from Phillips Exeter Academy, the prep school from which Zuckerberg graduated in 2002. It published its own student directory, "The Photo Address Book," which students referred to as "The Facebook." Such photo directories were an important part of the student social experience at many private schools. With them, students were able to list attributes such as their class years, their proximities to friends, and their telephone numbers.

Zuckerberg moved to Palo Alto, California, with Moskovitz and some friends. They leased a small house that served as an office. Over the summer, Zuckerberg met Peter Thiel who invested in the company. They got their first office in mid-2004. According to Zuckerberg, the group planned to return to Harvard but eventually decided to remain in California. They had already turned down offers by major corporations to buy out Facebook.

Walt Disney

Walt Disney was born on December 5, 1901, in Chicago, Illinois, to his father, Elias Disney, and mother, Flora Call Disney. Walt was one of five children, four boys and a girl.

After Walt's birth, the Disney family moved to Marceline, Missouri, where Walt lived most of his childhood.

Walt had very early interests in art; he would often sell drawings to neighbors to make extra money. He pursued his art career by studying art and photography and going to McKinley High School in Chicago.

Walt began to love and appreciate nature and wildlife, and family and community, which were a large part of agrarian living. Though his father could be quite stern, and often there was little money, Walt was encouraged by his mother and older brother, Roy to pursue his talents.

During the fall of 1918, Disney attempted to enlist for military service. Rejected because he was underage, only sixteen years old at the time, Walt joined the Red Cross and was sent overseas to France, where he spent a year driving an ambulance and chauffeuring Red Cross officials. His ambulance was covered from stem to stern, not with stock camouflage, but with Disney cartoons.

Once Walt returned from France, he began to pursue a career in commercial art. He started a small company called Laugh-O-Grams, which eventually fell bankrupt. With his suitcase and twenty dollars, Walt headed to Hollywood to start anew.

After making a success of his "Alice Comedies," Walt became a recognized Hollywood figure. On July 13, 1925, Walt married one of his first employees, Lillian Bounds, in Lewiston, Idaho. Later on they would be blessed with two daughters, Diane and Sharon.

In 1932, the production titled *Flowers and Trees* (the first color cartoon) won Walt the first of his studio's Academy Awards. In 1937, he released *The Old Mill*, the first short subject to utilize the multi-plane camera technique.

On December 21, 1937, *Snow White and the Seven Dwarfs*, the first full-length animated musical feature, premiered at the Carthay Theater in Los Angeles. The film produced at the unheard cost of $1,499,000 during the depths of the Depression, the film is still considered one of the great feats and imperishable monuments of the motion picture industry. During the next five years, Walt Disney Studios completed other full-length animated classics such as *Pinocchio, Fantasia, Dumbo, and Bambi.*

Walt Disney's dream of a clean and organized amusement park came true when Disneyland Park opened in 1955. Walt also became a television pioneer. Disney began television production in 1954, and was among the first to present full-color programming with his *Wonderful World of Color* in 1961.

Walt Disney is a legend, a folk hero of the twentieth century. His worldwide popularity was based upon the ideals that his name has come to represent: imagination, optimism, creation, and self-made success in the American tradition. He brought us closer to the future, while telling us of the past.

www.ingramcontent.com/pod-product-compliance
Lightning Source LLC
Chambersburg PA
CBHW032008190326
41520CB00007B/403